ON MEDITATION

ON MEDITATION

Finding Infinite Bliss and Power Within

SRI M

PENGUIN BOOKS

An imprint of Penguin Random House

PENGUIN BOOKS

USA | Canada | UK | Ireland | Australia
New Zealand | India | South Africa | China

Penguin Books is part of the Penguin Random House group of companies
whose addresses can be found at global.penguinrandomhouse.com

Published by Penguin Random House India Pvt. Ltd
4th Floor, Capital Tower 1, MG Road,
Gurugram 122 002, Haryana, India

Penguin
Random House
India

First published in Penguin Books by Penguin Random House India 2019

Copyright © Sri M 2019

10 9 8 7 6 5 4 3 2

The views and opinions expressed in this book are the author's own and the facts
are as reported by him which have been verified to the extent possible, and the
publishers are not in any way liable for the same.

ISBN 9780143447511

Typeset in Arno Pro by Manipal Digital Systems, Manipal

Printed at Repro India Limited

www.penguin.co.in

MIX
Paper from
responsible sources
FSC® C047271

To all the wonderful people
who made it possible for me to bring out this book

Contents

ON MEDITATION

ON MEDITATION

1

WHY SHOULD WE MEDITATE?

Q: What is 'meditation'?

M: Meditation is a very wide concept. The usage of the word 'meditation' in English refers to three of the parts of Patanjali's *Yoga Sutras*—*dharana*, dhyana and samadhi.

Dharana means the capability or the capacity or the practice by which one can put one's mind exclusively in one stream of thought. When that matures and becomes a continuous process, then that dharana becomes dhyana. When that dhyana can be sustained for a continuous period, then one can experience and understand what samadhi is.

Many a time, when a question like this is asked, a person is asking about a technique. All practices for meditation that are prescribed in the *Yoga Sutras* of Patanjali are included when we discuss meditation. The actual experience comes only with practise and this may be specific to an individual. However, practising the techniques is a good start. Patanjali describes this exercise of constant and continuous practise over a long period of time as *nairantaryaabhyasena*[1] and *dheerghakale*.[2]

When we can do this for a length of time with absolutely no distractions, then we enter into a state where we forget that we are even meditating. There is only that state. That is called meditation.

The object you are meditating on, the meditator and the process all become one. Once you experience this, all other definitions simply become techniques towards the goal. There is no reaching out or grasping. Just being. There is a cessation of all movement.

Remember, this can come about only because of the practise of a technique that has been taught. So, until you reach that point, the practise of the technique that has been taught to you, is what is considered meditation up until that time. And reading about it is not a remedy. While reading initially does help, regular practise cannot be compromised. You need constant practise over a long period of time, dheerghakale.

Now, a wonderful thing happens once you reach a certain stage in your meditation. Whatever you are doing, anywhere, in any situation, there is a constant stream of inner bliss, independent of anything else. This is something permanent and is what we are all seeking. This is what Omar Khayyam is alluding to in his *Rubaiyat*. Patience and one-pointed attention are required!

---

[1]   Continuous and constant practise
[2]   Over a long period of time

Q: Why should we meditate?

M: Let me start with a story which gives a clue as to what we are trying to connect with when we meditate.

Imagine that you're standing on the street and looking at the footpath. You see a man slowly walking along the street. He is old, looks very weak, with a bundle of clothes over his shoulder. You think he's some kind of a beggar, breathing hard and slowly trudging along. He looks as if he might fall on the ground and die at any moment. Now, imagine a bus coming, and at the last moment, the driver notices the man and brakes suddenly. The bus screeches to a halt blaring its horn; nine times out of then, this poor man, who you think cannot move another inch, who you think will fall over and die, will clear all long jump records when he sees that the bus is about to hit him.

The question is: 'How did he do it?' Somebody looking at the man from the outside would think he cannot move another two steps! He looked so weak and vulnerable! What happened to him when he suddenly faced the danger of the bus hitting him? How did he clear the long jump record from this side of the road to the other? That is the question.

There are many ways of looking at this. The first is, suddenly faced with a threat, he jumped. But where did this energy come from?

The second is a medical or biological explanation. In the brain, there is a section called the limbic system which is there to alert you and to make you react when there is a sudden threat to your life. It's a built-in feature of the old reptilian brain. So, when the limbic system is set into action, the man reacts. Specifically, there is a switch in the limbic system which suddenly pumps a large amount of adrenaline into his system. This adrenaline temporarily gives him the energy to jump. These are chemical and biological explanations.

The yogic or Vedantic explanation says that the man's past experiences up until this point have led to thought processes that made him think he is old, he is weak, he is going to fall over and die, etc. While these thoughts were constantly going on in his mind, at that particular time of danger when the limbic system set things into operation, he had no time to think. He had no time to think and condition himself with the thought that he 'cannot do it'.

Thought is a powerful weapon. It can be limiting and it can be un-conditioning, both! In this case, in his normal mode of existence, he puts two and two together very logically and thinks 'I was in the hospital six months ago; I'm weak in my legs and I can't jump . . .', so on and so forth. But, in that particular moment of danger, he didn't have time to think and condition himself to say 'I cannot do this'.

Thought can condition you and make you think that 'you cannot do something', and thought can also be conditioned to say, 'Yes, I can do it!' I'm not saying you shouldn't think; you should think. Don't put your thinking faculties in cold storage, especially when there are gurus roaming around. But in this case, to protect the body, a split-second of energy came from beyond ordinary thought. The energy said, 'Jump!' and the man jumped.

Now, that energy, which was accidentally triggered off in this case, can be tapped systematically and utilized for your life.

First, it can be used to un-condition the mind and make it more expansive, and second, it can be utilized to gain access to infinite modes of energy.

If thoughts such as 'I am this body', 'I am a man', 'I'm a woman', 'I'm a child', or 'I am an old person', can be un-conditioned, or at least set to rest for a while, then it's possible to access that source of all energy that is within us. Fortunately, this happens to be a blissful energy and not a painful energy.

From ancient times, for thousands of years, people in the East and the West, but especially in the East where people were more concerned with what was going on within, have discovered that there is an essence of all energy. There is an un-conditioned consciousness and bliss which is in all of us in the form of a little spark inside of our being, in the core of our being. The prerequisite for touching that is that you decondition yourself from the thought that 'I am limited', 'I am this body', 'I cannot do this' and 'I cannot do that'.

The conditioning process, on one side, is philosophical, and on the other side, it is practical.

There are practical ways of keeping your limiting thoughts in abeyance, at least for a while, and gradually increasing the time that you spend in an un-conditioned, blissful, super energy state. This is the practice or sadhana which is about how to zero in or go into the essence of this being. An essence which is not anywhere outside, but right inside us. An essence which is equally there for all beings, whether we have discovered it or not. An essence that can be touched through the practice of meditation.

Q: What are the different reasons why people meditate?

M: There are many reasons why people choose to meditate.

For some people, it's motivated by their desire to reach a goal. What happens when we really want something? We work hard and become deeply involved in our business or the work required to achieve it. Now, naturally, when we work towards a goal, obstacles come. When obstacles come, normally we face them, the obstacles are removed, and we move on. This is not only true in meditation, it is also true in everyday life. However, in this process, what happens when we don't reach that goal? Stress is automatically generated. When somebody or something becomes an obstacle to you achieving the goal, there is stress and there is conflict.

Hence it can be useful to meditate in everyday life to deal with this stress. If people don't meditate, they try to find some other form of entertainment—or alcohol. People drink because when they come home after a hard day of work, they often have a lot of stress and want to get rid of it. So they say, 'Let me relax for the time being and forget about the world!' When you drink, the senses are numbed, and you forget about many things, including the stresses from your day. You think you're fine, however the next morning there is a hangover, and then the next evening you repeat it. So instead of that, one can use meditation.

This is not the be-all and end-all of meditation. It is a good reason to start, but it is not the actual aim of meditation.

Others are motivated when they approach old age and consider death. They say, 'Well, I have been involved in materialistic activities for many years. Now that I've become old, I've got to think of what is going to happen next. There may be something coming soon, so let me get prepared for it!' They go around and visit various people to find out what can be done and decide, 'I want to be religious. I have missed it for such a long time. Let me start now.' They find somebody who says, 'Chant this mantra', and they begin chanting the mantra, or praying to

God in whichever form, and so on. Now this is another reason why people meditate.

Another reason one might meditate is when one walks into a place and they see monks, sanyasis, *brahmacharis*, ascetics, or religious people sitting down in meditation. When they look at them, they spontaneously feel a certain peace which they haven't felt before. Hence, they say, 'Let me also try and meditate and have this peace which these people are enjoying!'

There is also a very simple reason for meditation, where the family guru initiates you into a mantra and you always chant it because you think, 'If I leave it, perhaps something will happen to me.'

One of the most important reasons why one starts to meditate is when one day a person discovers that there is a whole circus going on around them. That this whole world they have built up around them has suddenly collapsed!

Sometimes this can come about automatically. Say somebody wants to make a million dollars, they work hard, and then on the final day, when their passbook has a million dollars, they come home and find out that the person who is dearest to them has died. Everything collapses. Then as a result, sometimes the desire to meditate comes automatically. Sometimes. I would say that it is good luck coming in the disguise of 'bad luck'. You'd think it cruel of me to say this, but it's a fact that sometimes the 'worst' things are good things that come in the worst form possible, because without that the human being would never turn or look to examine anything seriously. I'm not saying that it should happen, but I'm saying it does happen sometimes.

I'm reminded of a very interesting story about Krishna and Narada. Krishna told Narada, 'Let's go for a walk.'

Narada said, 'Alright.' Now, knowing Krishna, Narada thought, 'I'm going to be a little careful. I'll walk behind him and see what he's going to do.'

They walked and they came to a very rich man's house and Krishna said, 'Look, I'm feeling very thirsty. Can you go in and ask for some water?'

Narada said, 'Now, hold on! What are you going to do? What is the mischief you are planning? Tell me.'

Krishna said, 'I'll tell you that later. Let me have a drink! Really, I'm thirsty!'

Narada said, 'I'm thirsty as well, so let's both go in!'

Both of them went inside and asked for a drink. As soon as this rich man saw them, he thought, 'They are guests and guests are God!' So he said, 'Come and sit down.' He brought them some scented milk which they drank.

Then they got up and said, 'Thank you very much.'

When they went out of the gate, Krishna said, 'Now look, I'm going to bless this man.'

Narada heaved a sigh of relief. He said, 'He's going to bless him, fine. He's not doing anything else.'

Therefore, Krishna blessed him, 'May your health increase; may your wealth increase; may you be richer than you are!'

They had gone about ten steps when they came to a poor man's thatched hut, in a small compound with nothing else there except for a few pieces of cloth hanging on a line. Krishna said, 'I'm feeling thirsty again.'

Narada thought, 'Now there's something coming!'

So they went in and said, 'We are very thirsty, can you please give us something to drink?'

This poor man said, 'Okay, please be seated. I am engaged in doing some very important work. So, if you can just wait?' He went and bathed his cow. Except for the thatched hut, the cow was his only dearest possession. He wiped the cow clean, milked it and brought them some milk which they drank.

And then, when they went out, Krishna said, 'Now I'm going to "curse" this man!'

Narada said, 'My God! I knew something would happen! In your case, nobody can predict what!'

Krishna said, 'I'm going to curse this man! May his cow die!'

Narada said, 'What is this that you have done? He gave you milk from the only cow he had.'

Krishna said, 'Look, my dear fellow, you don't understand. Whenever I do something, you always think in the other direction. You see this chap's only attachment on this earth is this cow. I have to just remove it and he will come directly to me. I don't have to do anything else. But the other man will take a long time to come, so let him enjoy his wealth!'

What I'm trying to say is that sometimes, what you think is 'misfortune' is actually fortune which comes in the garb of misfortune. Only then do you begin to think seriously, 'Where am I going?', 'What am I doing?' Hence, that's another reason why people begin to meditate. When such things happen, then people begin to meditate, question, think, contemplate, because they have seen the emptiness of life.

There is another kind of person who meditates because they open their eyes properly, look around at the world and say, 'What is this? I'm enjoying the world, but this is going to come to an end at any point in time. I've seen so many things happen. It doesn't have to happen to me.'

Many people are happy, but most people are unhappy. I'm stating a fact which we generally prefer to cover up—I'm not being a pessimist. It's a fact that we suffer. Your suffering may be different from my suffering. But, the common factor is sorrow. And when I'm enjoying something, even then there is a hidden element of unhappiness there, because I'm afraid that the thing which I am enjoying might go at any moment. If I have common sense, I must know this—that I can't always enjoy everything all the time. I know that it will go, at some time. So, the moment I enjoy, there is already a hidden feeling of holding on to it, because it might slip away. And by recognizing this, a person may become motivated to meditate.

Apart from that, there are serious people who look at the world and see how temporary things are. They begin to wonder, 'Is there something beyond all this?' Then they go to teachers, read books, read scriptures. They come across scriptures that say, 'Yes, there is something beyond all this which is "permanent".' With the desire to find out, they start to meditate.

Now there is one reason why people meditate, which is very rare. A young child is born; when he is six years, he tells his mother, 'I'm going to meditate!' Now, we have no material explanation for this. There is an explanation but there is no meaning in going into this because, if I go into it now, if I discuss why her child suddenly takes to meditation without any known reason, it would just be theory. It means nothing. It is not a question of experience. Maybe there is something, some 'background', maybe there is 'some past life'. It's all theory, maybe, so it's better that we do not go into it for now.

Another reason a person meditates is because he or she spontaneously feels the desire to meditate, experiences a great joy in it and so continues with it.

So you have a rough idea of why people meditate, or, if people don't meditate, why they might want to meditate, or, if they didn't previously want to meditate, now they may like to try to find out why?

Q: Can meditation help with dealing with difficulty, health problems, sorrow or depression?

M: When you say meditation, people have different ideas about it, which is why you are asking me these questions.

Some people say they 'meditate to get well'; some say they 'meditate to find enlightenment'; some say they 'meditate to find wellness'; some think 'meditation can cure diseases physically'. Even to sit quietly and think about a problem is considered meditation. There are different opinions on meditating.

But, before we go into that, let's look at this word. Meditation is a word used in English which means many things to many people. If you go back to the Indian sources, the word meditation is actually split into three. There is dharana, there is dhyana and there is samadhi. All these three things put together is what we call 'meditation' in English.

Let's look at dharana. By the way, the question you asked may get addressed in the course of this answer when you look at it carefully.

Dharana means to be able to fix your attention on something exclusively without being distracted or disturbed by anything else. This comes through training and only through training, because our mind is usually in the habit of being distracted all the time. The reason that it is distracted is that it is disinterested in what you are trying to focus on.

The word dharana, which means exclusive, one-pointed attention, is something that happens naturally if you are seriously interested in the subject of your focus. If you are not interested, then it's not easy to do that. Then you need a technique to maintain focus. The technique is to fix your attention on the subject constantly, day by day, until one day it works. There's no shortcut.

Now, dharana is fixing your attention exclusively on something, can be an object, an idea, a sound, or an image. There are other things which could be added but these are roughly what you can fix your attention on. Whatever it is, it doesn't matter. Complete attention is very simple when you like something.

For example, there is a beautiful green and yellow finch sitting out there. When I first see it, the mouth falls open. You look at it and you are completely absorbed in one-pointed dharana of that finch, and not because someone is asking you to do it. Similarly, it depends on what you are seriously interested in. If you are seriously interested in enlightenment, then that enlightenment is like the finch that came and sat here. If you are not interested in enlightenment, then you are not ready for it. Then there are other things that you can work out.

If you can have dharana then you don't need to practise, it's there. If not, then you need to practise looking there all the time and try to figure out how to exclude everything else except the object of focus. For example, if there are several other birds that are also sitting around the finch, how does one exclude all the birds except the finch and focus on just the finch? When you can do this, it becomes a technique.

This is where yoga comes into the picture. Through practise, if that exclusive attention becomes continuous without a break, then, this is called dhyana.

Dhyana comes from the root *dhi*, which means 'to meditate'. When dharana becomes continuous, like when you pour oil from a vessel, then that *dhara*,[3] dharana, becomes dhyana. If you are seriously interested in a subject, then dhyana is automatic. If you are not, then through the practise of dharana, it stretches and becomes dhyana.

Okay, now the last word, 'samadhi'. Samadhi is when you are so absorbed in whatever you are looking at, that you totally forget yourself. There is no you. There is only that. This is samadhi.

You asked, 'Can it be used for physical health?' I can only say that if you are not well, if you want to give complete attention to that and diagnose what is wrong with you, if you look carefully, then it becomes dharana on your health. Out of that, will come a cure for it. Meditation need not necessarily be the direct cure. From dharana will come the idea of how to take care and then move forward.

Generally, meditation is applied to keep the mind quiet, because it is usually distracted, conflicted and running around. So, when you say meditation, dharana and dhyana, it is usually done to keep the mind tranquil, not only when you sit down but also amidst your daily life. If it only works when you sit down, it's a good thing; but if it also works when you are in this tumultuous world, then it is even better.

Now, the third function is enlightenment. In fact, dharana, dhyana and samadhi are an intrinsic part of the process to reach enlightenment. These three terms used are from the *Yoga Sutra* of

---

[3] Stream—a line of descending liquid like rain or water poured out of a vessel.

Patanjali, but they have been used in other forms, in other books, as well. These terms are specifically used in the *Yoga Sutra*.

Now, in the *Yoga Sutra*, what do they mean by 'enlightenment'? It means that they have managed to eliminate the distractions of thought like your disturbing mind and reached a tranquil state of mind where you suddenly realize that in your true essence, you are tranquil. That realization, you can call enlightenment.

When you say enlightenment, that doesn't mean you should always be sitting stiff. Enlightenment is enlightenment only when it's there, even in the midst of getting into a bus. It is always there. Therefore, since you have found peace and satisfaction, you really don't want anything more. But it's not as if you have become stagnant. In every minute of every second, it's renewed. That probably should be the ultimate use of meditation.

That said, it is also possible to use meditation to reduce stress. But these are temporary things.

Remember, the keywords are dharana, dhyana and samadhi. In samadhi, you are so absorbed, you have forgotten yourself. You are only *that*.

Q: What is mindfulness?

M: 'Mindful' is a beautiful word. Now that it has come into the mainstream, people everywhere are trying to think about it. I am very happy about this. In fact, for the last two years, I have been going to the Google office in the Bay Area to address employees, because they now have a full-fledged mindfulness chapter. Yahoo has also invited me. In fact, when I went to Yahoo, I tried to explain to them what 'Ya-Hoo' actually means. It's very interesting. It's a little bit on the side but it has interesting connections.

There used to be a sect of Sufi mystics in the caves of Syria and there, they used to practise a certain type of pranayama or breathwork, which is similar to how you chant 'Om'. Their sacred sound is 'Whoo'. When the Oriental researchers went there, they found this group of people sitting in the cave saying 'whoo, whoo', and so at first, they named them the 'Howling Dervishes' because they were howling like wolves. But, according to the Sufi teachings, the 'whoo' is actually the last sound of the Arabic word of 'Allah-hoo'. In Arabic, 'Al' means 'the', and 'lah' means 'no'. It's a negation. So, Al-lah means 'the no'. It's very close to the Buddhist concept of *shunya*, nothingness. So, it is 'the no'. But then, when you add a 'whoo', it becomes 'the nothing but "whoo"'. So, these people sometimes shouted 'whoo' and sometimes shouted 'ya'. 'Ya' in Arabic means 'oh!'. So 'ya-hoo' means 'oh-whoo'.

In Melbourne, the other day, we had a talk at the Theosophical Society and the subject was 'Mindfulness and Beyond'. When you say 'mindfulness', it means a sort of meditation where you are mindful of every thought and you are mindful of your breath. The Theravada Buddhists call it vipassana, being mindful of your breath. The breath is there from birth to death, but we don't give it any attention, yet it's so important for our survival. You can be without food or water for an extended period of time, but you can't be without breath for half an hour. The moment you begin to give attention to your breath, you become mindful. You are inhaling, you are exhaling, and your mind becomes completely connected to the breath. That's one kind of mindfulness.

The other kind of mindfulness has to go side-by-side with internal mindfulness if we need to move forward spiritually. That mindfulness is to be mindful of the outside world, of what we speak, of what we do, of how we treat people. I can sit and talk about peace, then go home and mistreat my wife, what does that mean? It means that I am not being mindful. When there is mindfulness inside, it is reflected in mindfulness outside. Or, rather, if you begin to develop mindfulness outside, you also develop mindfulness inside. Which is why all the great teachers say there are some rules and regulations. Follow them.

Let's look at outer mindfulness. You know how we create problems just through words? Be mindful of what you say. Be very careful. For example, here I am talking to you and it appears as if it's effortless, but actually, before I say anything, I am weighing my words carefully. Do my words affect someone negatively even though they may be true?

Words can cause a great deal of problem. Sometimes you can hit somebody, you can slap somebody, and it may be forgotten in a day or two, but if you use words which hurt the person, he or she might carry it for life. So therefore, when you speak, watch carefully. This is very important in your spiritual life; it's not that you simply have to sit down and meditate.

Eighty per cent of the problems in this world, which are connected to internal problems, can be avoided if we follow three principles of mindfulness: First, I should consider what I am going to say before I speak. I should give it a thought, half a minute, think about 'What am I going to say?'

Two, who am I going to say it to? Sometimes what I am going to say may be okay, but the person I am going to say this to may not be the right person. For example, going to somebody who believes that so-and-so is the last prophet and saying, 'No, no, there is another prophet!' It may be true, but I can't say it to that guy, right? It creates immediate trouble. So, first, what am I going to say, and second, to whom am I going to say it?

Third, is this the right situation to say that? You may be saying the truth, you may be saying it to the right person, but what if he just had a fight at home and then you say this to this person? It may come with a different reaction. So, we can't always be 100 per cent right, but as far as possible, if we can look at this, many problems can be avoided when we operate with mindfulness inside. I know, you may say, 'Who's going to bother, just lead your life', but then we go around again and come back in the same circle and say, 'Now what?' I do think that it's possible to change, forget all the past that has happened and look at the present so that the future is good.

Therefore, there is inner mindfulness and outer mindfulness, and to live a mindful life is to integrate the two.

A person who is mindful is usually a gentle person, because the mind has settled down. You cannot even goad such a mind to get angry with somebody, it's not possible, because the person sees that the other person is not different from himself or herself. The person sees that in reality there is only One.

Then why do we see multiplicity between us and others? Because the mind is split into pieces, as though it's cracked. There is conflict, there is confusion. It thinks, 'I want to do something, but someone else is not letting me do it; I really don't want to do something, but someone else is forcing me to do it.' This starts with childhood.

For example, you have a child who is interested in music, but you want him to become a doctor because doctors make a lot of money, what do you do? You force him into medicine. I am not saying this is the case for everybody. One specific example that comes to mind is a lady who is a doctor in Long Island, New York. When she was young, she was fond of music. Her parents were both doctors and they wanted her to become a doctor, so they pushed her into medicine. In India this happens quite often. She is a very successful doctor now. In a situation like this, some people can turn that regret into anger and violence, but she did not; lucky for her, she got herself a nice piano, and in her free time she plays and listens to music. She says, 'The best times in my life are when I play the piano.' This is a demonstration of resolving the problem, the problem that results from the mind being in pieces where we want something but get something else due to our circumstances.

Now, when you are able to see that the root of the mind is one, that these pieces are artificial divisions of the mind, when you see that the mind is calm and quiet, aware of itself, when it is mindful of the outer and inner and also mindful of the breath, then the mind slowly starts to integrate. You soon begin to see that there are no pieces, no separation of you and me, that there is only one mind, one whole.

You might think what I'm saying is metaphysical, but it's actually quite logical. When I say, 'We are one, that the mind is one', you might respond and say, 'No, my mind is different, his mind is different, how can the mind be one?' So, let's examine this more closely.

I might be angry about something and you might be angry about something else, it may not be the same thing. I might be jealous of something, you might be jealous of something else. I am afraid of something, you are afraid of something else. They may not be the same things for each person, but what's the common factor? Fear, anger, jealousy. It may also be goodness. I might love someone, the person may be different, but the common factor is 'love'.

If you look at this carefully, the emotions are the same for all human beings. The objects may be different, but the emotions are the same, they are the common factor.

I am saying that there is only one mind, which has been artificially split into different characters, different personalities, into different parts, but where these characteristics are common across the board. Based on this logic, if we hypothetically agree that it is so, then if there is a small change in one end of the mind, in you, then it must reflect in some way throughout the entire system.

Let's look at some examples. In a negative situation there is a person, a powerful person, who through the strength of his thoughts can influence the collective mind. Through that influence, he can send thousands of people into the gas chamber. One person. On the flip side, one good person can influence thousands of people and say, 'Bless them that curse you.' It's a tall order, it's not easy.

Every now and then, you will find an individual who has hit upon this truth, that there is one mind. They may have discovered it consciously or unconsciously, but they hit upon the truth that you and I are not separate, that there is one mind. They've discovered that if we tweak it on one end, it's going to be reflected on the other end.

Therefore, those of us who want to be mindful should be aware of this fact. Furthermore, if you want to make the world a better place, you can go out and reform it as much as you want. But, if you don't change in here, in your heart, if you don't become mindful of your inner nature and realize that the mind is a common factor between all of us, then, however much you reform the outside, the problem of violence and war cannot be solved. We have to start by changing our own heart, here. We have to be mindful.

If I am in the midst of war in my mind, how can I deal with the war outside? Can I drop my arms and be peaceful inside? If one person does this, it can affect a number of people. Hence, we should start within.

Therefore, mindfulness is outside, and mindfulness is also inside, and if both these can be integrated, that is called mindfulness. If this is done, then it's a stepping stone to go beyond, beyond the ordinary mind.

Since we are on the subject of mindfulness, I want to share a small story. It's not a story, it's something true, but if I tell it like a story it sounds better, because everybody enjoys 'once upon a time'. Jesus used parables.

We did a 'walk' through the length and breadth of India where we walked 7,500 km from Kanyakumari to Kashmir. Not only myself, but many of us walked together. Prior to this walk, I had an opportunity to meet his holiness, the Dalai Lama.

I was quite taken aback by the humility of this man. He is a Nobel Prize winner, a universally recognized figure with millions of followers, but when I went to see him, he was standing near the door with his secretary, and he put out his hand and said, 'Welcome, come inside.' I was nobody and I was much younger than him, it wasn't required of him, but why would he do that? Mindfulness. You mind your actions, you mind what you do.

We went inside, and I was worried about where to sit or whether to leave my shoes on. So, I said, 'I am taking off my shoes,' and he replied, 'But I am wearing my shoes.' We sat down, he sat here and

I sat there—you might see it on YouTube. Then he took out my autobiography in English, which somebody had already given to him and he said, 'I need a signature on this.' I signed the book, he took it and he touched it against his forehead, because it's about Himalayan Masters and so on, and put it away.

His Holiness said, 'Okay, so you are going to walk?'

I said, 'Yes.'

He asked, 'But why? You will be so tired when you finish the walk!'

Then I responded, 'But I think I need to do it, I have a reason behind it.'

'Yes, yes, I know,' he said, 'many great people have walked, the Buddha walked and so on. You know, I can't walk, I have very bad knees.'

I thought, perhaps he thinks I have come to ask him to join the walk. So, I clarified, 'Your Holiness, it's okay, you don't have to walk.'

'Yes, good, okay so you are determined to walk? Do it!' he said.

I replied, 'Yes.'

He said, 'May all the bodhisattvas bless you.'

I thought the discussion had ended there. There were lots of people waiting outside, diplomats and others, so I started to get up, put my hands together and said, 'See you, Your Holiness.'

He responded, 'But where are you going?'

I said, 'There are a lot of people outside waiting for you.'

'Nobody is waiting for me, so please sit down.'

I sat down, and we got into a discussion. I talked with him about the Upanishadic concept, that the supreme reality which we seek is everywhere. I said that the Upanishads say, '*Tad dure tad vadantike*', which means that 'it's far and yet so near', and wondered whether this, which was being explained in Vedanta, was the same in Buddhist teachings when they say shunya.

So I asked him, 'Does shunya mean nothing?'

'No,' he responded, 'Shunya is that from where the whole world comes and goes back to, so it can't be nothing. But it is not a "thing" either.'

'The Buddhist expression is shunya,' I said, 'and in the Vedantic expression it's *purna*, "full". Two ways of looking at the same thing. You can call it shunya, because no words can describe it, which the Upanishad also agrees, *yadvachanaabhyutitam*—which words cannot describe. You call it shunya, we call it purna.'

He said, 'Yes, I think we meet there.'

I continued, 'But then the Upanishad says something very peculiar, it says, "*Yanmanasana manyute*"—even the mind cannot conceive of it.'

He said, 'If even the mind cannot conceive of it, what is it to me? I have no other instrument! Let the Brahman be there, I am here, and that's the end of it.'

I thought about it, and responded, 'Your Holiness, from my understanding, I think what it means is that the ordinary mind cannot understand it.'

He said, 'Yes, so you have to be clear about it, the ordinary mind cannot understand it. But a mind that is mature enough can understand it.'

'That's probably what it means,' I said.

'That is called compassion,' said His Holiness, the Dalai Lama.

So this is what happens when you are really mindful. True mindfulness and true sensibility take you beyond that which can be defined. This is mindfulness and beyond.

2

HOW TO MEDITATE

2

HOW TO MEDITATE

Q: How should one meditate?

M: I must deal with this one by one.

Different kinds of people conceive of the divine in different ways. Some people like to conceive of the supreme energy as God with a form. Others think of it as an energy. The Buddhists say shunya. There are Christians who like to think of the manifestation of the supreme energy as Jesus Christ. Among the Hindus, who have thirty-three crore deities to choose from, people may think of God as Devi, or as Shakti, or as Ganesh, it doesn't matter. And some think of it as an all-pervading supreme reality—Brahman.

There are different modes in which people like to look at divinity and it doesn't matter which mode you choose. But to reach the goal you can't simply say that, 'I am all-pervading, unconditioned, free, and if I think about it, I will reach there.' You can think about it, of course, but you need to find the way to reach it.

Earlier, we were talking about dharana, dhyana, samadhi as a path to reach the goal. This is because you need to learn how to fix your attention on *that divinity*, and not just say that divinity is what you are. It's very dangerous to say that 'I am the Brahman' because the ego becomes very strong. It's better to say, 'I'm not this, but maybe when everything ends, then there is the Brahman.'

Humility is essential.

Affection is essential.

Fellow human beings should be given value.

To begin the meditation, first sit down and decide which form or what mode you would prefer to connect with that energy inside. Once you decide that, the next step is to bow down.

This is important. There's nothing wrong with bowing down, okay? You are not bowing down to any person. You're bowing down to thin air. Some people say, 'I don't want to bow down to anybody.' But there's nobody in the room! Bow down. Touch your head to the ground and let it be grounded and grateful. Be thankful for your existence on this earth, that you have food, clothes, a place to stay. Be thankful that you have a family—or that you don't have a family— both are good. You can say, 'Thank you I don't have a family, I'm free.' Or you can say, 'Thank you, I have an understanding family.' Either way, be thankful to this earth for providing everything that you have. You don't have to use Sanskrit, you can say 'thank you' in any language. No problem, God is a linguist.

Now straighten up and sit in a comfortable position. When I say comfortable position, it means that different positions are comfortable for different people. For me, it is sitting cross-legged. Traditionally, according to the yoga shastras, the cross-legged position is very good for meditation. There are many reasons for that and I won't go into all of them, but it's related to the energy channels in our system, which are called the *ida, pingala* and *sushumna*. Sitting cross-legged helps adjust the energy levels, the prana and *apana*, which flow through the *nadis*, the energy channels.

It's nice to sit cross-legged, but make sure you are perfectly balanced and erect. Being erect doesn't mean that you need to be tense, it simply means that your body should not be slack. Don't sit as if you're sick. Sit properly, be alert, yet be relaxed and comfortable. If you can't sit cross-legged, you can sit in a chair, but if possible, try to keep one foot up, like *dakshinamoorti*.

While in the sitting posture we have different methods of meditation, in which the body has to be tensed a little bit before it can relax. If it's not tensed, there is no way it can relax. In my tradition, the Nath tradition and the *kriya* yoga tradition, we do something called *mahamudra*. Given below is a simple version of mahamudra.

If you are sitting cross-legged, you can bend down. Hold the knees with your hands and try to touch the floor with your forehead. Hold it there and then straighten up. Do it a few times so that your whole system is nicely stretched. If you do this three or four times, you will notice that when you sit up, your body is more relaxed. It is relieved from not bending.

Now sit in a comfortable posture and turn your mind within. There is a simple method to bring your mind from outward distractions and turn it inside. This method can be practised by anyone no matter which religion you practice or what way you look at divinity—with form or without form. Anyone can do this.

The method is to give total attention to your breathing. Everybody has a breath, right? Prana, or breath, is there for everybody, it is a common factor for everyone. The Gita says '*prana apana sama yukta*', equalize the prana and apana. How do we bring the prana and apana, which means the upper breath and the lower breath, together into balance?

Now this technique I'm going to give you is free. You don't need any chequebooks. It's a fashion these days where if you don't pay then you don't get. But it doesn't apply here.

Sit down and take a deep breath. The first question that arises is, 'How do I take a deep breath?' There are different ways of breathing, and in this instance, we are looking at the yogic breath. The yogic breath is not surface breathing where you screw up your nose. No. The yogic breath is deeper. In yogic terminology, this breathing technique is called *ujjayi*, where you're not breathing as much through your nose, but breathing through your throat. How? I open my mouth and breathe; however, instead of inhaling with my mouth open, I do the same process with my throat, but where my mouth is closed. The air is flowing through the nostrils, but it's going in in a much deeper manner, touching the throat centre.

Next, when you inhale, chant mentally. You can't chant out loud because then you would not be able to practise the breathing. When you breathe, mentally chant the sound of 'Hum'. Or you can imagine and visualize that when you're inhaling, the inhalation is Hum. It's very easy.

Breathe deeply. Don't breathe in jerks, but breathe in slowly. Hold in your breath for half a minute and then start exhaling.

Now there are two ways of exhaling. You can either exhale deeply with your mouth closed or you can exhale with your mouth slightly opened. When you breathe out, imagine that you are chanting the sound of 'Sau'. So, when you breathe in it is Hum, and when you breathe out it is Sau.

So exhale. This is similar to when you are tired, and you've been out walking or running, you come home and sit down. What is the automatic response when you sit down? You sigh 'Aaahhh!' and exhale. This exhalation clears all the carbon dioxide. Do this exhalation deliberately.

Breathe in, mentally chant Hum, hold it for half a minute, don't stress it, and exhale either with your mouth closed, or slightly open, mentally chant Sau and allow it to go. Hum. Interval. Sau.

In terms of how many times you should do this, just do it for ten minutes. Keep a timer or a watch, I don't want you to count. And don't worry too much about the breath, about how it goes or where it goes, just take it in, hold your breath, and breathe out.

At the end of ten minutes, you will discover for yourself that things have calmed down. You will notice that you're not as distracted by things outside, and your mind is enjoying itself in the Hum and Sau.

At this point when the mind is calm, there are a couple of things you can do depending on your orientation. Those who think of the divine with a form can visualize that form inside the heart. For example, if you like to think of the divine as Shiva, then you can think of a white or black linga inside your heart and chant the relevant mantra. The chanting of Hum and Sau is now over, so you may chant the mantra that is suitable for the visualization. If the divine form is Shiva, then you chant 'Om Namah Shivaya'.

If there is no form, then you can chant the sound of Om. One way of chanting Om is called *bhramari*, which means the bumblebee. You know the bumblebee that comes to the window and makes the buzzing sound?

With bhramari you use your thumbs to close your ears, and then chant Om. You do this with more stress on the last sound, the 'm'.

'Ommmmmmmmmmmmmmmmmm.' Watch your mind and chant the sound of Om. Allow the sound to vibrate in your head. Do this for five minutes. Since you can't chant Om for five minutes with one breath, take another breath. Keep your hands on the ears, take a deep breath and start again.

While you do this, as you hear the sound of bhramari vibrating inside, fix your attention on the middle of the forehead. How do you fix your attention on the middle of your forehead? You have nails right? Knock a few times in between your eyes. 'Knock and it shall be opened unto thee.' So knock, fix your attention on that point and make the sound of the last part of Om. Let it vibrate inside your head and continue to do that for five minutes.

You've done ten minutes of Hum and Sau, and five minutes of vibrating the sound inside or chanting and visualizing God in your preferred form.

Now drop everything. No bhramari, no Om, no God with form, no Hum or Sau. Just sit quietly. When you sit quietly, sit with the understanding that when everything is still, the essence of your consciousness is the only thing that *is*—which is your true identity. At this point if you hear rain or the birds, don't try and cut it out, it's all one, it's all a part of us. There is no difference. We have learned to differentiate ourselves with time and space, but it is actually limitless.

Sit quietly. Sit as long as you want. If you follow all the practices carefully, you will find that when you sit quietly, you're actually enjoying something wonderful. Enjoy it as long as you want, or as long as you can. Once you are done, once again bend down, touch your forehead to the ground, and say, 'Thank you.' In my lineage we chant 'Om Sri Gurubhyo Namaha'. Or you can just say 'thank you'.

You can do this practice fifteen minutes a day. It's not a tall order if you really want to do it.

I've given you a practice which is practical and has no denomination. You don't have to convert into this or that. Whoever you are, you can do it.

Q: We often hear about the importance of meditating on the chakras, especially the third eye, the ajna chakra. Why is that?

M: This is in relation to the science of yoga and the science of tantra, both of which are interlinked. When I say tantra, don't think of orgies in the cremation grounds—it's gotten a bad name but it's not like that. In fact, if you want to see the real link between yoga and tantra, there's a beautiful text called *Sat Chakra Nirupana* which goes into this. This text has been translated by a Britisher, Sir John Woodroffe, who was a justice in the Calcutta High Court during British times. He got so interested in these matters that he left the judiciary and wandered off with the tantrics to learn from them. He wrote the wonderful book, *The Serpent Power*, under the pen name of Arthur Avalon.

According to *Sat Chakra Nirupana*, in yoga and tantra, there are different centres of optimum energy in the human body. There are seven centres that are known as chakras. Starting with the bottom of the spine, the bottom centre is called the *muladhara*. The word *mula-adhara* means root foundation if you translate it literally. The next one is between the navel and the lowest chakra— it's called the *svadhisthana*. Then there is the *manipura* which is in the navel, the *anahata* at the centre of the chest, and the *vishudda* in the throat.

Then there is the ajna, which is in between the eyebrows, also known as *bhrumadhya*, and then there is the *sahasrara* which is on the crown of the head.

The whole theory of tantra and yoga is that energy operates in all human beings, but normally on the gross level. This energy is considered the feminine energy, Shakti, which has traditionally been represented as female in India. When this energy acts in the lower centres, that's more than enough for our daily existence, for food, for sex, for everything. When the energy is very active in the muladhara centre, some people can be highly sexual. The libido is the same energy, but it's at the gross level.

The *tattva*, element, for the energy of the lowest centre, muladhara, is called *prithvi*, which is earth. I think translated properly, 'prithvi' means solid. As we go up, the energies turn subtler and subtler and subtler. When we get to the next centre, svadhisthana, the energy is considered to be *apas-tattva* which means from solid to liquid, symbolically showing that the energy is moving from gross to subtle. When it comes up to the navel, the manipura, the element is *agni*, or fire. Now, when liquid is heated by fire, then it becomes vapour, so the next tattva is *vayu* for the anahata.

These are all symbolic, okay? There is no vayu here. These tattvas illustrate that our awareness is being lifted from the gross to a heightened state of the subtle.

Now the ajna is an important centre. When the energy reaches the ajna chakra, it reaches the turning point where the subtle energies take over and the gross energies diminish. Another reason this is an important centre is that according to yogic anatomy and physiology there are three nadis which are the ida, the pingala and the sushumna, which are said to cross each other at the ajna chakra and go in opposite directions to the left and the right brains. Hence the ajna chakra is an important energy centre, which if you meditate upon, you go deeper within. Now if you draw a straight line inwards from the middle of the forehead, a little above the eyebrows, and you draw another straight line down from the middle of the crown of your head, the point where the two lines meet is where the pineal gland is.

The ajna is an important centre, which when activated, one can ascend from the lower to the higher. Even in the Gita when Krishna talks about *jnana yoga*, he says you should fix your attention between the eyebrows.

That said, there is another important centre which is the heart. When I say 'heart', I'm not referring to the organ that pumps blood, I'm referring to the core of your emotions. When you get emotional, you usually feel it in the chest, you don't feel it in the head. These two centres, anahata and ajna, are both very important from the yogic point of view.

Q: Can meditating on the third eye distract one from the real purpose of meditation?

M: No, not if you do it properly.

When we say 'third eye', we're not referring to a physical fact, we are referencing an inner opening, an activation in a certain area of the brain, which is physically connected to the ajna chakra, also known as bhrumadhya—between the brows.

From my understanding, meditating on the third eye can never be a distraction because it can always lead you deeper and deeper and deeper if you do it properly. However, for those who are more spiritual through an emotional connection, the heart centre, the *hridaya*, is a good place to go. Ultimately, when your energy and awareness go higher and higher, they have to eventually come here (points between the eyes). You don't have to press for it, you don't have to push, it comes—so it can never be a distraction.

That said, you should learn it from an appropriate person who knows what they are teaching you. One simple technique, if you want to feel what it is like, is to take a feather and rub it slowly on the forehead between the eyes. You will feel a ticklish sensation; once you experience this, just focus your attention on the sensation and sit down. Don't imagine anything. Just sit. The feeling is more important than the visual.

Q: What is the importance of visualization in meditation and how can we utilize this?

M: I think when the Bible says God breathed the breath of life into Adam—it is talking about the capacity to visualize. It's a symbolic way of saying that a certain capacity, which is divine, has been added on to the human being, to the mortal. It is this capacity of imagination and visualization which has allowed the human mind, humankind, to improve, evolve and to reach this state.

We build great cities, great businesses, make great medical discoveries, and all this is possible because of imagination. Albert Einstein is on record as saying that imagination is more important than even knowledge. Because the secret is, if you can put your mind into an idea which you want to achieve with complete visualization, as if it is actually there, and if you can do that constantly where you know a technique by which that can be done, then believe it or not, sooner or later, it becomes a reality.

There are exceptions where it doesn't work. But there are explanations as to why it doesn't. That is a different matter. For the time being let us think only of that which can happen and not that which doesn't happen.

The secret of the visualization, of creative thought, is to actually believe and to visualize. To picture the details of what one wants as if one is already there. When this is done, the subconscious mind carries it to the higher level, which we could call, at the risk of criticism, the super-conscious mind.

The super-conscious mind responds by giving ideas to the brain on what it should be doing to achieve that which it wants to achieve. It is an ascension of one's plans to a higher sphere and it is a descent of energies to the ordinary mind—well, you could call it blessing— so that one achieves what one normally could not have achieved.

For that, one has to first set the mind free from its conditioning, from its prejudices. One of the most important keys to this is to say, or to affirm regularly, that my knowledge or my understanding of any situation, including myself, may not be perfect. It may be that there are many more layers to it. Perhaps there are more dimensions to it. I can see only a few angles, but perhaps there are infinite angles.

In order to understand this, the first step is to open the mind. When the mind is open, and when there is a great desire to achieve something, then the channels for achieving it are opened.

There is a descent of great energy which cleanses the mind and opens it up to receive what it has been asking for.

If you ask me, 'Is there a technique to do it?' I would say, first it is a question of attitude. Once the attitude is clear then you have certain practices which help to free the mind from prejudice and open it up to receive higher energies which are infinitely more creative than you could have thought of. I am going to describe one of them.

It need not be a religious practice, you can consider it merely as a mental exercise or a psychological technique.

First, get away from your place of work or the place you are accustomed to in your day-to-day affairs. Even if it's just for a few days, even two days. Go to a new place—the more beautiful the place, the better this is going to work. Try to find a place where there are plenty of trees and where there are birds waking you up in the morning. Or, where you can see beautiful mountains from the window. Or the seashore, where you can hear the waves dashing against the banks, against the shore. Go to a place like that.

Shut off your cell phone, or if you like, keep it on for an hour or so a day so that you don't keep worrying about what has happened out there. Eat light food so that you don't have to work hard to get food. Shut off the TV and pull off the plug.

Now find a place to sit. It could be on the bed or it could be on the ground, but the important thing is that you are not disturbed by anybody. If you are in a resort or a hotel, put up the 'Do Not Disturb' board on your doorknob.

The important thing is that you should be able to look out the window at the wide open world. Sit near a window and sit in a comfortable posture—you could sit in a chair, sit cross-legged, or in *vajrasan*, which is called the prayer position. Then start with your eyes open and take a look at the world outside. If it is raining, look at the rain, if there are clouds, just follow the clouds. For the time being don't expect to get anything out of what you see. Just see, just be.

'Have fewer thoughts' is what I am trying to say. Listen to the sounds that you hear outside. Make sure that the room is well ventilated and leave the window open.

Then take a deep breath. While you breathe in, think of or visualize the beautiful, free, fresh energies of the earth, of the world in which you are, entering your body and into your lungs while you breathe in. Since you are sitting in the midst of greenery—green itself is a soothing colour—if you like, you can visualize breathing in beautiful green vapour, which is coming into your lungs and filling your body. Stay with it. Let it fill every little part of your body.

You are now like a part of the beautiful paddy field that may be in front of you. Lovely, beautiful, tranquil, green, wide expanse which is you, inside your heart. Then visualize that there is a beautiful light glowing there, in the heart. The light is quiet, tranquil and calm, not raging like fire, it's like moonlight. When you breathe out, visualize that all the negativity in you, all the limitations in you, are slowly coming out of your nostrils and are being wafted away by the wind. When you have done this a few times, inhaling and exhaling, you are then left with no impure substance, but just that beautiful energy which is around you, inside you and all around. When you have done a few rounds of inhaling and exhaling, let your breath become normal again.

Now, close your eyes, and once again fix your attention on that beautiful calm moonlight inside your heart, and say to yourself, 'I am no more the old person, I am expanding, I am growing, I am de-limiting myself. I refuse to be confined to such small spaces; I am flying, soaring like a bird into the wide open spaces. May I be helped to reach great heights. May my mind expand. May my mind not be confined to a dark cell, may I be free, may I be free, may I be free.'

After having said this, open your eyes, and once more look all around. You will notice a new glowing character to everything outside.

Get up, stretch your legs, take a few steps and sit down again. Now visualize what you want to achieve with every detail as if you are already there. If you want a beautiful house, think of it in detail—think of the house, the furniture and your favourite sofa in which you are already sitting and relaxing and looking out of the window. Do this every day in the morning, and before you go to sleep. Believe it or not, you will achieve what you want to.

But there are many factors that can hinder this. One is, you certainly won't go anywhere if you are prejudiced and keep saying, 'No, no, no, I am doing all this but I don't think it will happen.' Then it's better that you don't try.

This is one of the ways to set the mind free. To move out from the normal weather-beaten track and to go out into the open expanses. To be free and to soar like a free bird.

Q: You have mentioned a meditation where you pray to your guru, imagine his padukas—the feet—and a flower. Can you explain this more?

M: It's always good to get help from a spiritual teacher.

There are many spiritual teachers; if you look at their faces, then you distinguish this teacher from that teacher. One may think of Shiva, another may think of Ramana Maharshi, and another may think of Padmasambhava Guru Rinpoche. Instead of worrying about the face of the teacher, we can just think of the padukas. If you think of the feet, then the face is not associated. The Ultimate Reality is the real guru. No personality is involved.

Now, meditate on the feet of the guru, the padukas. Padukas could mean feet; it could also mean footwear such as sandals, which the sadhus or teachers wore in ancient times. Keep the padukas inside your heart.

Then you close your eyes and touch your heart with your hands and chant 'Om Sri Gurubhyo Namaha' which simply means 'Om, I bow down to the guru'.

It's also a nice idea to say, 'I have no enemies.' Throw some flowers around and then sit down. Think good thoughts and then close your eyes.

Now, take a deep breath and as you inhale, chant Hum. You may also say Om. When you inhale, the mouth is always closed. Once you inhale, hold it for half a minute, no sound, nothing. Then, exhale.

When you exhale, chant the sound of Sau. There are two ways to exhale, one with the mouth closed and the other with the mouth slightly open. So, when you exhale, chant the sound of Sau.

Say Hum and Sau as slowly as possible. Not fast, that is different. Get your mind to go with the inhalation and exhalation and stay with it as long as you can. End it, when you think it's time.

If you do it seriously you will feel 'I should have done a little more'. You will begin to feel something nice going on inside. But then, you have to stop somewhere, right? So, deliberately say, 'Stop now, I have to go to work' and then bow down and touch your forehead to the ground. Bow down to the guru's padukas and say 'Om Sri Gurubhyo Namaha'.

Q: I am very devotional, is there a way to meditate for those of us who love God with form, as Krishna, Hanuman, Kali, etc.?

M: Bhakti comes to simple people who are devotional in their temperament, where they have a personal relationship with God, and they cannot conceive of a God without form, one who is without shape.

People like you prefer to have a personal concept that your minds can relate to. This is called bhakti yoga—the yoga of devotion. Now, don't think that the 'yoga of devotion' does not have meditation in it. Meditation is a part of bhakti yoga, because what does the devotee do? He or she first selects the form of God which appeals the most to them and then, when the selection has been done—Krishna, Rama, Buddha or any other—the mantra which is applied to that particular God form is given to this person and then he or she begins the actual chanting of mantra. *Japa*, chanting of a mantra, is also a very important form of bhakti, of devotion.

In bhakti yoga, when japa is to be done, one conceives of a lotus or a flower, or a light in the centre of one's chest or heart, and then, one invites that form of God that one has selected, to come and reside in there. After that one begins chanting the mantra, which is a form of meditation.

Another option is to follow the example of a devotee who is totally absorbed in singing the names or the glories of God in whatever form they have selected. There the meditation is automatic, because the mind is automatically diverted towards that.

Q: I have heard about Vedantic meditation. Can you please elaborate?

M: There is, what is called, 'Vedantic meditation'.

In Vedantic meditation, it helps to have a preliminary calming of the mind by pranayama, by watching the breath or by japa. After you have calmed your mind, then the intellect becomes very sharp.

Even the great authority of *Advaita Vedanta*, Adi Shankaracharya, had prescribed pranayama as *nadi shuddhi*, clearing of the nadis. He felt that when the nadis or the channels were cleared, then the intellect also became sharp and the mind became subtle enough to understand the truths of Vedanta.

Vedantic meditation is mostly to do with your thoughts and your mind.

How does it come about? Have you opened your window and by accident, suddenly noticed a full moon on a beautiful night? And for a few seconds you forgot everything except the moon? You did not exist for those few seconds, only the beauty of the moon was there. This is a form of Vedantic meditation.

In Vedanta, what the Vedantist does is to examine the world around him and find that it is impermanent. He says, 'This world is impermanent because today it's here and tomorrow it is gone. All the joys that I have are bound to disappear when I die. Nothing is permanent because anything that is born is bound to die. So, this is not the truth, because the truth has to be something that always remains, and has no tinge of sorrow in it. It is absolutely blissful and is not affected by any of the changes that are taking place around the world. This has to be the truth that I am searching for.' So, he says, 'This is not the truth.' This process is called '*Neti, neti*'. 'This is not the truth; this is not the truth; this is not the truth.' Thus he negates.

This form of meditation, I would say, is one of the most important and most effective forms of meditation, because by completely fixing his mind on the thought of trying to discover the truth, his whole attention, all his faculties, everything, is on one point. The mind is very calm and very subtle. It is taking out things one by one and saying, 'This is not the truth; this is not the truth; this is not the truth.' It is going from gross to subtle—something like an onion—you peel off each layer till you come to the centre.

You see how much attention is to be given to this? Total attention.

Then he comes to the conclusion that he himself is not the body or even the mind with which he has wrongly identified himself. So he goes deeper into his being, saying, 'If I am not the body, if I am not the mind, then, what am I?'

This process of self-discovery in Vedanta is what is called Vedantic meditation.

Now, to help with this there is one other form of meditation which is meditating on one's own thoughts, which means, carefully observing your thoughts.

Sit down and close your eyes, or leave them open, it doesn't matter. Invariably, many thoughts will automatically come in. Now, feel that you are there as a witness who is watching these thoughts. There's nothing to imagine—there is an actual witness watching these thoughts! Thoughts come and they disappear. Sometimes you start with one thought and it stretches on and connects to something else which is totally different to where you started.

When you watch this whole process, try to discover where it originates from. How does it start? Just watch the thoughts and try to find out where they start from. How do they come into being? How do they disappear? Because they are not always there. They are so volatile that they come, they move and they disappear. Just watch it and see how this whole process is taking place. This is also Vedantic meditation.

To temporarily understand a state of mind where thought has completely ceased, there is one other form of Vedantic meditation, which is to sit down quietly and imagine that your mind is like a sharp sword. Then, as each thought comes into your mind, imagine that you are cutting it off immediately.

This is very much applied by the Mahayana Buddhists. It is part of their yogic discipline. In their meditation, they cut every thought as soon as it comes. It's a mental process where, when a thought comes, you cut it off. Naturally, another comes, you immediately cut that as well, and this whole process of cutting off thoughts goes on and on and on, until at some point there is a split second when there is an interval between one thought which has vanished, and the other which has not come in. This is what they are looking for!

Once they grasp that, they have grasped what they are looking for—because that is the essence of one's own self, one's own consciousness which remains without being affected by any of the thoughts that are spun around it.

This centre of consciousness is within oneself and all who have experienced it have declared with one voice that it is a blissful experience—not an ordinarily blissful experience, but a totally blissful experience.

The *Mahanirvana Tantra* says, '*Anantam Anandam Brahma*', which means that anandam which has no *antah*, no end, is Brahman. And that comes about only when the thoughts have ceased, which means, the whole process of thinking has ceased. This is not unconsciousness. One cannot achieve or attain it by becoming unconscious. It's simply that one goes deeper and deeper into one's consciousness, and all the illusions we have about being this, and being that, all these illusions are being removed little by little until one comes to one's real source of being, which is called *atma*.

Q: Can you guide us on how to meditate on the breath?

M: In meditation you first start with being aware of your breath.

The breath is a very important link to that which is beyond. If you want to move from mindfulness to that which is beyond, the breath is a real, real link to that.

Let's start by looking at the idea of the breath. You can live for many days without food. Mahatma Gandhi lived for so many days without food. You can live without food for many days. You can live without water for some days. But you cannot live without breathing for half a minute. You can, if you are a yogi who is neither breathing in nor breathing out, but usually, half a minute is the maximum time you can go without breathing. So breathing is the most important thing in life. And when it goes, we are like a flat tyre, we are dead.

The breath is so important, yet we are never aware of it. We think that it is quite natural, the way it is going on. The breath started before birth, in the womb, and it goes on until it stops, and then we are dead. But we are not aware, we don't give enough attention to it. The breath is the link between me, between you and that from where the breath comes.

There is a beautiful statement in the Old Testament, where it says that after making the image of Adam, God breathed his breath of life into it. Now this breath of life is prana, energy, not just in your lungs, not just where the wind goes in; it is your life force.

Therefore, when you understand and become aware of your breathing, aware under all circumstances, not just when you sit down, you will notice then that your mind becomes settled and goes deeper and deeper into the inner layers. This is called awareness of breath—it is called mindfulness or watchfulness.

In the Theravada Buddhist teachings, not the Mahayana, though I have nothing against the Mahayana, but in the Theravada Buddhist teachings, the only exercise which Buddha is supposed to have prescribed is called vipassana. It has now become a brand, but vipassana is to be aware of your breath while you meditate. It is to be aware of your breath and give it a little attention for a change. Just as you give attention to your food, your drink, your actions, give a little attention to your breath.

Let me explain this a little more. For example, if you are very agitated about something, and then you remember that somebody suggested for you to watch your breath, when you go back and be aware of your breath, you notice that while you are agitated, your breathing pattern, the rhythm of your breath is very agitated. However, watch your breath if you are listening to beautiful music, or doing something you really love. Watch your breath perhaps while you paint—I am saying this because I paint sometimes— or while you are practising music or some kind of dance, but not the rigorous kind where it looks like you have been bitten by the tarantula spider. When you do something that you really love to do, revert to your breath and watch it. The breathing pattern will be calm and quiet.

So, the rishis, the ancient teachers, said that if there is a link between your emotional state and your breathing rhythm or pattern, if a change in your emotional state affects the rhythm of your breath, then you can change your mood using the breath.

Watching your breath automatically calms it down. If you can be aware of your breath, if you are mindful of your breath, you don't have to do anything, except watch it come in and watch it go out quietly. You will see that, after a while, the mind calms down.

If your mind is already purified, if you don't have hatred towards anyone in the outside world, and your emotions are under some control, then from there one naturally ascends into a higher state of spiritual experience.

If the mind has not yet been purified, then it subsides into deep sleep. Both are not possible, but something definitely happens. Either sleep or a calm higher state of mind. In order for the breath to slow down, you don't have to say, 'I will breathe slowly.' You just have to be aware of it. Be mindful of your breath. Watch it coming in and watch it going out. And if you do that for a while, automatically after some time you will want to take a deep breath, like a sigh, a deep sigh. Everything will become calm, quiet and will slow down. Now, when the breath slows down, and you are aware that it has become quiet, it will feel as if the tempest is over and there is a calmness, the calm after the storm.

When you are there, you will begin to be aware of inner things which are not related to the outside world, such as inner sounds. The first sound you will probably hear when the breath becomes calm is something like a drum or a thumping sound, which is your heartbeat. You normally cannot hear it without a stethoscope, but when your mind is calm and you are watching your breath, then you can hear, dub, dub, dub, dub.

As you go deeper and deeper in your awareness of the breath, there comes a time when the breath becomes so slow that it almost ceases, almost. It doesn't cease completely, because the body has to be maintained, but it becomes very slow, and then you begin to hear sounds which in yogic terminology are called *anahatshabd*. This means 'sound which comes without striking two things together'. '*Ana-hat*' means 'without hitting' or 'without striking'.

This inner sound is likened to clapping with one hand. Given that you need two hands to clap, this is almost impossible to conceive of. One way we can conceive of clapping with one hand is to imagine the inner sound which comes, not from two physical objects hitting each other, but from the inner movement of molecules, the inner movement of prana.

Hence, there is an inner sound, which is the anahat sound. As one fixes one's attention to that, sometimes, not often, but in a rare instance you may even hear beautiful music coming from inside. Or sometimes when everything is quiet, you might hear something, such as crickets even when there are no crickets outside. If you hear that, please check if there are crickets outside, it might be that they are there. The other day somebody told me, 'I have been meditating the last six days and I can smell some beautiful perfume.' I said, 'Please check if the lady next door is wearing perfume.' You must be practical about these things. However, when you have ruled out all that, then you feel something special happening, special feelings inside. These can be felt by being aware of your breath, and as you become more and more aware, your mind goes deeper and deeper, it even goes beyond sound.

Then you come to the essence of your being which neither breathes in nor breathes out; when that is reached, usually your breathing is very, very slow. You don't have to stop it. It's not a forcible stoppage of the breath, that is *kumbhak*, which also has its effects, but is a different phenomenon. When the mind has settled down, when everything is quiet, this calmness is the beginning of what Patanjali describes as *chitta vritti*, the cleaning up of mind stuff. The stopping of all the *vrittis*, all the waves.

When these waves stop, when the mind is calm and quiet, there is no you or me, there is no meditator or the meditated upon. When this happens, that's the take-off point, or the tarmac from which you take off to higher levels of consciousness. It's not the end, because there are many layers. But that's the take-off point from which you go to higher levels of consciousness. Unless that state is created, it's not possible to ascend to the higher levels, however we may chant or meditate.

Q: Can japa be a form of meditation?

M: Yes, japa is a simple technique by which the mind can be brought under control, for some time, and made quiet. This is a simple form of meditation which is useful for people who work and are thinking all the time about their work. As I said before, the most important part of meditation is that the mind must become calm. Without the mind becoming calm, there is no meditation. So, how does one go about it?

The simplest meditation is one in which a sacred word or a letter or a sound is given and the person is asked to repeat it. This is called japa. Even if one is not religiously inclined, it can help in ordinary life to bring yourself under control, to keep your mind calm, to keep you free of agitation and tension.

There is nothing hidden or esoteric about it. But, it is advisable that one gets the mantra from somebody who knows about it. A mantra is simply a word, a sound, a letter or a sentence which is given by a teacher to a student, who is supposed to chant it regularly.

There are three forms of chanting.

One is loud chanting. It's always good to begin with chanting loudly because you can hear it yourself. There are people who say, 'I like silent chanting. I don't like loud chanting.' But, what happens is, when you chant silently, after sometime, your eyes are closed, your chanting is over and you are thinking of something else! Now, when you chant loudly, this doesn't normally happen because you can hear your own voice.

When you become perfect in the discipline of chanting loudly— and by 'loudly' I don't mean like a loudspeaker, I mean 'audibly'— then you can begin chanting with just lip movements.

Finally, you will be able to chant without moving your lips, mentally, which means you imagine you are hearing the chant going on.

Now, there's a very simple mantra which anyone can chant without getting initiated by anybody, which is Om. You can just chant Om. Or there is another mantra, Sau Hum. You can chant, Sau Hum. Then, there is the Gayatri mantra which has been there for hundreds of years.

Hence, japa is one way of calming the mind because without the mind being calm and quiet there is no meditation.

Q: Should we try and maintain silence?

M: We cannot maintain silence. It comes and goes on its own. Neither you nor I can maintain or retain it. The moment you try to retain it, there is conflict. When it comes, enjoy it, live with it. When it goes, leave it. Don't even try to hold it, however miserable you feel about it.

What does love really mean? It is separation. When your beloved is with you, there is no feeling of separation. When the beloved is not there, the pining for *that* is called love. It is pain, but an enjoyable pain. Why do people sometimes enjoy sitting in the evening with a small glass of whisky in their hand and listening to K.L. Saigal singing '*Jab dil hi toot gaya*'? What is this feeling? It means that they are enjoying that pain. So, when it comes, be with it. When it goes, leave it. Let it go. It is not something which we can ever control. Really, we cannot.

Isn't whatever we see around us, just *that*? In some form or the other? Again, let's not get caught in forms. There is no difference between form and no-form here. The energy is everywhere, the wind, the earth, the plants, in the growing and becoming of the plant. All this is a part of *that*. We cannot really differentiate and say it is this and that. But when we stay with it, when we are quiet and that stillness strikes us, then we are in it.

Stillness comes, it doesn't speak—stillness can never speak, it is a wrong word. How can it speak? It's a contradiction. So, when it comes, then you are in it. When it goes, nothing can be done about it. To understand that one cannot do anything about it, is humility and worship.

Q: I am of an emotional nature, what role does feeling have in meditation?

M: Without deep feeling nobody would even step into spiritual enquiry. Feeling is known in Sanskrit as *bhava*. Bhava matures as we progress in meditation and in the spiritual path. In spiritual matters, bhava means a deep feeling of wanting something which you cannot find in the ordinary world.

It's like a child who particularly wants to have some chocolate. You can give that child anything else, it will just throw it away, because it wants only chocolate. On the spiritual path, that feeling, that one-pointed bhava, is the bhava to find the truth.

This bhava is a deep feeling. These are not merely intellectual matters. Intellect can go up to a certain limit, but if you take the intellect, which of course is the best instrument that we have, beyond that it becomes dry intellectualization. There is nothing left. You can go on saying things like 'this world is maya', 'this is reality', but you don't really know.

Hence, bhava is required to find the truth. Feeling is required. Without feeling, it becomes hard to fix your attention on something and meditate. Why do people say it's hard to meditate? It's because they don't have a liking for that thing. That's why they cannot fix their attention. If I love a flower, if I have a bhava of love towards the rose, I don't need to 'try' to fix my attention, it is automatically fixed there. Therefore, feeling is very important in meditation.

Now, a little bit on the scientific side. Today, neurology has advanced to such a level that they can map or scan parts of the brain even while you are awake or doing an activity. When they scan the brain, it has been found that when a person has what you call a spiritual experience, it is not a logical experience, but rather, it's the intuitive side of the brain which is active.

Brain scanning shows that when a person is in so-called deep meditation or a trance, like a samadhi state, it is the limbic system that is active, which is the centre of feeling. It is the limbic system that tells us to act when there is danger and it is the limbic system that decides feelings. It is the centre of feelings in the mid brain, where if some part of the mid brain is removed, if the limbic system is removed, then the person will end up as a mechanical being with no feelings.

Hence, experiencing feeling at an anatomical and physiological level is an important part of meditation.

Now, most of us have had a dose of Darwin, right? You must have been taught about 'the survival of the fittest', where unless you are fit you cannot survive biological evolution? But let me ask you, when you were a small child, did you have any freedom or any will to survive because you were fit? Or were you helpless? The child is helpless. It is not fighting to survive. It is the parents who look after the child. Hence, I think that one of the key phases of evolution is helplessness.

Similarly, bhakti, the highest state of bhava, is when you declare that 'I am completely helpless, so please take over.' It's all in God's hands. We realize that however much we think we can, we are truly helpless. That is bhava. That is spiritual enquiry. Not that you shouldn't do anything.

Bhava is something that has to come spontaneously. And we have enough proof to say that this bhava is there in every human being in potential form. Now, it has to be seen whether this bhava is directed towards searching for that which we have lost, the truth. It is there, but it is usually directed in other directions like when a mother looks after the child; or when the child is physically separate from the mother but the mother is very much in love with the child; or afterwards, when the child grows up and falls in love with somebody. However, after all this bhava has been satisfied, if the mind is still yearning for something else, that is called spiritual bhava. It's an unfulfilled feeling that comes in the heart, and you are pining for it.

Even in tantra, when the main energy is activated, it is supposed to bring about different changes in bhava within a person's mind, and takes him to the higher dimensions. This energy is the same energy which in most human beings acts as sexual energy. When it operates only through one centre, the bottom-most centre, it is sexual energy. However, this same energy, which is full of feeling, when awakened and made to ascend to the higher levels of healing, of consciousness, is supposed to bring about a total change in the consciousness of a human being, a transformation. It is feeling. And it is essential for this spiritual search.

That feeling is awakened in different people in different ways. When you are a devotional type of person who likes to sing and dance, then that feeling is created by singing and dancing in prayer. If you are a yogi who is sitting down in *padmasana*, the lotus posture, and doing your exercises, the same energy is awakened. When it is awakened, there is feeling.

In fact, it has gone even to the extent where certain great sufis and *bhakta*s like Chaitanya Mahaprabhu have said that the bhava is even more important, more valuable and more enjoyable than the fulfilment of the bhava. One story is that Chaitanya Mahaprabhu was pining to have a vision of Krishna; pining, meaning his heart was breaking, but when Krishna appeared, he said, 'Now why have you come, it was so sweet, that pining for you!' That is called bhava.

So, feeling is very important. Bhava is essential on the spiritual path.

3

MEDITATION POSTURE AND PRACTICE

Q: Does it matter what time of day we meditate?

M: The first thing I suggest is set apart some time in your daily routine where you can sit by yourself and practise. This is very important. There are some people who believe that to sit and try to meditate is a conditioning in itself. Forget that idea and put it on your bookshelf. You need to have some time to sit down, a fixed time if possible. The reason for this is that everything comes through habit.

People say you should break a habit, but that should come later—first we need to develop the habit in order to break it. For example, there is a classical Indian dancer, and people say, 'Oh she's wonderful, she innovates so nicely.' But how can she innovate if she can't dance? In order to innovate she needs to know what classical dance is. She cannot simply go on the stage and wave her arms around. Therefore some structure is necessary to start with before you can break it. Pick a time and don't budge from it. Don't say, 'I should take the dog out for a walk this morning.' If that's the case, either change the time for walking the dog or change the time for meditation. I also have dogs and take them for a walk.

When it comes to fixing a time, early morning is good—the earlier the better because things are quiet and activity has not started yet. The only sounds you hear may be the birds chirping outside, which is nice. If you meditate and you hear the birds chirping, don't try to cut them out, they're part of the whole 'thing'. You and they are not so different. Except that the early bird gets the worm, and the child asked the teacher, 'But who asked the worm to get up so early?'

Early morning is a good time to sit down, a beautiful time, where everything is still quiet and the energies have not yet been dissipated by activities. I'm not saying you should wake up at 3 a.m. and sit. According to tradition, *Brahma muhurta* is a beautiful time for meditation, it starts at 3.30 a.m. Don't try that, because then you will go to the office and sleep. But find a time, perhaps early in the day.

If for some reason you cannot do it in the morning, come back and do it before you go to sleep. Have an early dinner and don't practise on a full stomach. If you have had a meal, leave an hour or an hour and a half. If you have had a little bit of alcohol, then don't do it that evening. Do it the next morning when you're free of the alcohol. It happens nowadays, the doctor might ask you to have a glass of wine because of your heart, but sometimes we don't stop at one. Sometimes it becomes two, or three, then you can't meditate.

Q: What should I wear when I meditate?

M: I suggest for those who seriously want to meditate, that you have a set of clothes which you use only for your meditation. The reason is, whatever you wear carries your traces in it. The clothes also carry traces of the mind or the actions carried out while wearing them.

For example, if you're somebody who works in a mechanical shop, you wear your overalls. You don't wear overalls and sit for meditation, because if you wear them you will feel like doing mechanical work. You know what I mean? It's all associated. Its vibration or its association, we won't go into that, but it is there.

Therefore, have a clean set of clothes, they need not be fashionable, nobody needs to come in and see what you're wearing. But it's important that you have something comfortable. It's difficult to wear tight jeans and meditate, especially if you want to sit cross-legged. I have nothing against jeans, you can wear them at other times.

Q: How should we sit when we meditate?

M: Sit in a comfortable position. When I say comfortable position it means that different positions are comfortable for different people. I prefer sitting cross-legged, *sukhhasana. Sukha* means happiness and comfort. Traditionally, according to the yoga shastras, the cross-legged position is very good for meditation. There are many reasons for that, I won't go into all of them, but it's related to the energy channels in your system, which are called ida, pingala and sushumna. Sitting cross-legged helps adjust the energy levels, the prana and apana which flow through the nadis. Nadis are the energy channels. It's nice to sit cross-legged, but make sure you are perfectly balanced and erect. Being erect doesn't mean that you need to be tense, it simply means that your body should not be slack. Don't sit as if you're sick. Sit properly, be alert, yet be relaxed and comfortable.

There are many other postures in the yogic system as well. You can sit in *siddhasana*. If you change it a bit it becomes *svastikasana*. There is vajrasana, which involves putting your legs back. Another meditative posture is *veerasana*. There is *gorakshasan*. Then there is the classical 'Buddha pose' known as padmasana, or lotus posture.

Q: What if I can't sit on the floor without back support?

M: If you can't sit on the ground, you can sit on a chair, but if possible try to keep one foot up, like dakshinamoorti. Now the question is 'What if I have a problem with my knees?' or 'What if I have a problem with my back?' How am I supposed to sit? Lean. Take a pillow, lean, take the support of a wall or sit on a sofa that doesn't sink in. Lean. *'Brahma leen'*. When a great yogi dies or a swami dies, he is supposed to merge into Brahman. The Sanskrit word for 'merge' is 'leen'. So they say 'Brahmaleen Sri Swami Satchidananda Saraswathi'.

So if you can't sit this way, then you need to lean. But be practical. Don't say I can't meditate because I can't sit in padmasana.

Q: If someone is injured or can't get out of bed, is it possible to lie down and meditate?

M: There's nothing else they can do. Gradually they should try and sit up and meditate if possible. When you sit up the movement is different than when you lie down. The spine is horizontal for most animals who walk on all fours, parallel to the earth. We, humans, have vertical spines, perpendicular to the earth. This has something to do with the meditative states. It is a good idea to sit.

If someone is paralysed and they feel that they can meditate, if they are lying down, it is good to help them lean a bit. If they are uncomfortable then you can bring them back to the supine position. You can also meditate lying down but lying down is usually reserved for sleep.

Q: When someone is meditating, what should they do with their hands?

M: One thing is clear, when someone is meditating they are certainly not twiddling their fingers. In fact, when you are seriously meditating this question doesn't arise because your hands know exactly what to do and where to rest.

That said, if you are just starting out and you want to know how to proceed, the best thing is to keep your hands in a position where they are comfortable and relaxed. If you are sitting cross-legged then the best thing to do is to put your hands on your knees. Or you can cross the hands together.

They say that if you cross the fingers then the circuit, the movement of energy, is completed. I have tried, and I think either way is okay, as long as it is not uncomfortable. What is required is that there should be minimal effort, as long as you don't raise your hands in the air. The classic yogic pose is to fix your index finger with your thumb and sit down.

If you feel that you are supplicating and asking for something from God, then you can sit with your hands open and palms facing upwards.

I think each individual should try different options for a while and figure out which is best for him/her.

Q: If your heels don't touch your lower abdomen in padmasana, is it okay?

M: It is not required. In fact, too much touching at the lower abdomen may cause a hernia. I had a problem myself. People like to do this because they think the ida and the pingala are closed. While this is true in hatha yoga, you have to be careful.

Ida is the channel (nadi) on the left side of the body. The breath that travels through ida is considered to be cool like the moon.

The pingala is in the right side of the body and is considered the channel for the hot breath, like the sun.

Tha is the sound symbol for the ida and *Ha* is for pingala. Control over these is therefore called hatha yoga.

Q: Should I meditate with my eyes open or closed?

M: You can meditate with your eyes opened or closed. Some people can't meditate with their eyes closed; the moment they close their eyes the mind starts whirring, full of chatter. If that's the case, then open your eyes, look, and for some time do nothing. Can you sit just like that, doing nothing whatsoever? Don't think, 'Oh that is a nice pine tree. I can build a roof with it and then profit from it.' Then desire comes in and your mind is no longer quiet.

Q: After practising around thirty minutes of any sitting asana, the legs sometimes get numb. What is the solution for this?

M: After practising an asana for thirty minutes, the legs begin to ache and become numb. What is to be done? One simple solution is to unfold your legs, stretch them and come back. Gradually you see that the duration of your meditation increases. That is one way of doing it.

The other is you don't worry about your legs becoming numb, they are not going to become paralysed. Get that fear out of your mind. After some time, little by little—and don't try too much in one go—continue with the discomfort and don't do anything. First, the legs will get numb, then the torso with become numb, then the neck will become numb, then the head will become numb. When all things are numb, one day you will find yourself standing over there looking at this.

We get so worried about this numbness and then we immediately move because of the discomfort. When an entire system becomes numb then you are out. YOU are out. The shell is numb.

In fact, some yogis sit for long hours in *paschimottanasana*, with their legs stretched forth, holding the toes and bending down. We have a similar exercise in kriya. If you do paschimottanasana properly then your head is on your knees and your hands are holding your feet.

I know a yogi who used to sit in paschimottanasana for eight hours. One day when I went and poked him, he was not there, his body was sitting in paschimottanasana, but he was not there. So the next day I asked him what the matter was. He replied, 'You know when I do that, the entire system gets numb after some time, and I'm out. I saw you yesterday coming in and poking me.'

It will take time. No point in coming out of the body as long as your desires are still intact. What is the point? You will come back again. Better to go slowly.

Q: Do you require a very healthy spine? If this spine is not in proper shape, will it hinder?

M: The spine is a physical extension or symbol of the inner spine which is the sushumna. It is always straight. You must keep your spine as steady as you can, there is no other way.

All the nadis that we are talking about—ida, pingala, sushumna—even though they have their physical counterparts, they are actually psychic. The ganglionic chain on the left and right are ida and pingala and are the outward projections of the inner subtle body. We have a physical body, we have a subtle body and we have a still subtler body. Let's not get into this, as it goes on and on.

Since we're on the subject, when the awareness of consciousness lifts from the bottom-most centre to higher and higher on the spinal level, we are actually changing our thought process in our mind from the ordinary solid, to liquid, to vapour, to air, to vayu and *akasha*. That is why the lowest centre, muladhara, is represented by the prithvi tattva. Prithvi means the solid world, the three-dimensional world; actually it means a cube which is the primary image for three-dimensional reality. It's at the ground level. That is enough for most of our functions in this world.

When it goes higher up to the svadhisthana, it enters the world of liquid, which means the subtler world, from solid to flowing. When the heat, the fire of the manipura, is applied to it along with the sound *Rum*, then that heat turns the water or the element of apas into that of vayu which means air. So, the mind has now become very subtle, from the physical to a vapour in the anahata. Higher up is akasha.

Akasha is the original essence of undifferentiated matter, from there comes the undifferentiated atoms, *anu*, in the form of invisible sparks. I don't know if you are aware of this, but no human eye can see an atom. We only know it exists because of its reactions; you cannot see it with your eyes. And beyond that, you cannot see anything.

Anu is an ancient word, which means the smallest point of matter, a spark. Hence, you are lifting your consciousness, or your awareness, from the gross, to the subtle, to the subtler, until you reach the subtlest. Beyond that is akasha which cannot be grasped by the ordinary mind. There, you put up your hands and say, 'My God I don't know.' Similar to Arjuna after the eighth chapter of the Bhagavad Gita when he saw the *vishwaroopa darshana* and said, 'Oh God, I don't know.' He said, *'Tvamadi-devahpurusah purana'*, as there was nothing else he could utter! He saw a man who until now was sitting beside him, patting him on the back and saying, 'Hey, hello friend, how are you' and then suddenly turning into something ungraspable.

The potential for that vishwaroopa is in every one of us in seed form, in *beeja* form. That is what we need to touch. Wherever there is a manifestation of great things, great glories, even in the physical form, in the material sense, such as great heroes, it's always a tiny manifestation of that seed, because of which all this happens.

So what happens when you touch the source? It's bigger than Hiroshima or Nagasaki. While that was destructive, this is constructive. Thousands of megatons of energy—shakti.

Q: When one meditates, and the body relaxes, often one may need to pass gas, burp, go to the bathroom or yawn. Is it okay to pause and do these things?

M: Yes, if it's becoming uncomfortable and one needs to pass some gas, then get up and do it. If you are alone then you can do it right there. If there are others in the vicinity, then go out as there will be sound as well as air pollution which will disrupt the meditation of others. Also, if you need to go to the toilet then you should go. I mean you can't do it on your asana.

Yawning is all right, you don't have to move anywhere. When you yawn it means your brain needs more oxygen. When you yawn you take in a lot of oxygen and a lot of carbon dioxide is expelled. One way of dealing with yawns is to do *pranams*, touch your head on the floor a few times so there is more oxygen in the brain. Yawning is okay, as long as you don't yawn into someone else's nose.

I also know of many people who complain that when they go into a deep state of meditation they feel like burping. I know people who sit down to meditate and then belch. They can't control it. They say it only happens when they sit down for meditation. It's better to burp than to hold it in. I went to one ashram where they were doing some kind of yoga. Many people were sitting and belching. It's not pleasant but when the burp comes it's better to burp, not hold it in.

Q: Why can't I meditate after alcohol if it relaxes me?

M: Alcohol messes you up. What we are aiming at is to have clarity, right? Alcohol paralyses the central nervous system, so there cannot be clarity.

When we meditate, we are not seeking a stupor, rather, we are seeking a calm tranquility and clarity, and alcohol interferes with this. There is no harm in having a drink, but don't do your kriya or meditation after that. This doesn't mean you should drink in the morning if you want to meditate in the evening. I personally think that a glass of wine does no harm to anybody, it's vegetarian, you don't kill any animals. But, you have to be careful because it is addictive.

The challenge with alcohol is when you can't do without it. No human being should be dependent on anything. You shouldn't say, 'I can't do without it.' If you can carry on without being dependent, great! While people start that way, they can often become dependent.

I know wonderful people who have a drink every day. They are not bad people. We cannot say 'Oh these fellows are bad.' There is no sense in that because I also know people who don't drink but are terrible fellows, what do you do about that? But for your own good, it's better to control or avoid, if possible.

The other thing is when we drink from that which is inside us, we don't need to drink outside. There is an intoxication which can be produced within us which is very healthy, not addictive, good for the liver and so on.

Q: Can we have a cup of coffee before meditation?

M: Absolutely! Coffee is allowed, tea is allowed. While coffee and tea are fine, cannabis is a no-no. Sorry!

4

EXPERIENCES IN MEDITATION

Q: What experiences do people have when meditating and what are the signs of progress in meditation?

M: During the process of meditation you may start to experience lights, different colours coming in, the smell of flowers and sounds.

When a person begins to meditate, what happens is that his mind becomes subtler and subtler. So, when the mind becomes subtle, it is able to sometimes sense, see, hear or smell things which would normally not be possible for the grosser mind to be aware of.

When these lights are seen or sounds are heard, it helps the person feel, 'Something is happening, perhaps I'm advancing', and therefore, he sticks to it and goes on. Otherwise, if nothing happened, he might say, 'What is this? I've been meditating for so long and nothing is happening to me.' So, these are some signs on the road.

Of special importance is the hearing of sounds, because once you begin to hear sounds, then it becomes easier to meditate. The

sounds are generally musical. They are called *shabd*. In fact, there is a
school of yogis who call it *surat shabd*, inner sound. Once you begin
to hear the sound, then it's very easy for the mind to fix itself on that
sound, and simply listen to be carried into deeper states.

These are the signs that come and go. But since they are signs
on the road, they should not be given too much importance, because
there are other signs on the road as well! If you are going to Shirdi,
it is better not to tarry too long at Dharmavaram—have a cup of tea
and push on!

There are other signs of progress as well, which aid in keeping us
on the path of meditation. The best sign of you progressing in your
meditation is something which is very self-evident. Nobody has to
tell you that it's happening. First is the experience of great bliss; and
the second is the actual experience of your being, not just a little
thing but a throughout expansion of being in all ways. Not merely a
physical expansion, it's an expansion in all forms, in all ways. This is
the important thing that is experienced.

When we have a real experience of the conscious self, it is
something which needs no external evidence. Once one has it, there
is no question of any doubts creeping in there, because it's a total
certainty; it's as certain as you are sitting here now!

Now I must tell you something very, very important. Long ago,
when I was with my Master, we were travelling around and one day
I told him that I must learn to meditate six to seven hours every day
without batting an eyelid. He turned to me and said, 'I can show you
many examples. However, if you can meditate ten hours a day and
continue meditating for ten hours a day for ten years, but you cannot
hear the cry of a hungry child next door, then all your ten years and
ten hours of meditation are an absolute waste.'

What this implies is that when we say we are meditating, we are trying to evolve spiritually, the first sign of spiritual evolution is not that we are able to levitate in the middle of the drawing room. Or that we can cure somebody of all diseases. Or that we can sit for six hours with our closed eyes without moving a toe. Those are not the signs of spiritual development. The sign of spiritual development, a major sign, even the initial sign of spiritual development, is that one's heart begins to thaw. If a person says he has gone into deep samadhi and is seen to have the same stone heart, then that means that meditation has not really worked.

What is it that we are ultimately meditating for?

We are meditating under the hypothesis that every living being is a spark of the divine. You cannot start to prove something without a hypothesis, right? You need a hypothesis, then a theorem and then you prove the theorem. If you cannot prove the theorem, then that theorem is wrong. So we begin with the theorem or the hypothesis that deep within every living being is a spark of the divine. It may be covered for various reasons, it may be hidden, inactive, not manifest or not kinetic. But all living beings must have that divine spark, and we cannot be the only ones exclusively carrying that spark.

Therefore the aim of meditation or spiritual practice is to discover that, by going deep within and touching that divine spark in us.

Now, if this hypothesis is correct, then when I discover my spark, I have discovered the spark in others. It cannot be otherwise. Once I have discovered this, then care and compassion for others is a natural outcome of my recognizing my identity with the other person. Nobody is different. Everybody is the same, deep within. Outside, of course, we are different. We all know that.

Hence, the first manifestation of going closer to this spark is that we begin to understand that we are a part of the whole, that we are a part of the whole universe and that every living being is a spark of the divine. In fact, the very movement in meditation is towards that.

Therefore, if we are serious about moving towards the spiritual goal and meditating, then we should act and live in this world as best as we can. We should try our best to be kind, both when it is easy and when it is tough. This will be different for different people, so you have to watch yourself carefully. Observing oneself in a relationship with others is a very important part of spiritual sadhana.

I'll end with an example. I have said this before. If I go and sit in a cave in the Himalayas and meditate for thirteen years and at the end of it I say, 'Now I am really free of anger, free of sorrow, free of jealousy', and so on, it actually makes no sense, because in the cave there is nobody to get angry with. I cannot get angry with the cave. I cannot get jealous of anything there, because there is nothing to be jealous of. It's only when I come out of the cave and into the world, when I board a bus from Rishikesh to go to Haridwar and somebody steps on my toe in the bus, that is when I know if I am really free of anger, jealousy, etc.

Therefore perhaps one of the most important markers of spiritual progress, of progress in our meditation, is how soft our heart is, whether we feel the pain of others, our care for others, not just our family but for everyone.

Q: Sometimes one has certain spiritual experiences. Is that what 'enlightenment' is or is that a different state that one can get into at will?

M: With regard to spiritual experiences, glimpses of certain experiences we refer to here are certainly not what you get through the sense organs. One may experience something in an altered state of consciousness. Perhaps for a short while, there may be an instance of great bliss or a feeling in one of the energy centres. One may hear a beautiful sound or see a light sometimes at the ajna, between the eyebrows. Sometimes there is an activation and we may experience quietude and a wonderful, never-before experienced feeling.

In order to address the second part of the question about enlightenment, we need to bring in clarity about the usage of these words. People have many ideas attached to the word 'enlightenment'. Many of us think enlightenment is something that happens all at once, and then there is freedom forever. Even if that freedom is forever, we do not really understand what it means because we have never been free from everything. We have only been free from one problem or from another, but never free from all problems.

If we look at this carefully, it is found that the reason we are not free from all problems, all at once, is because the problem actually comes from 'me'. As long as 'I' am there, there is no complete freedom.

Enlightenment is certainly a blissful experience, otherwise, nobody would move towards it. In fact, every human being, whether they want to know God or not, whether they believe in God or not, deep down in the inner recesses of their mind they want to move towards *that*. In some way, the whole of evolution is actually a movement towards happiness, total happiness, the kind which we all want but unfortunately don't get.

We become happy with one thing but there is something else which is missing. We try to grab this and that too disappears. This is normal existence and if you watch life you will see this whole activity.

Now this unceasing activity of trying to grasp, and that object continuing to evade us, is called *samsara*. Samsara is the wheel of life and death in this world, and this cycle keeps the world going. It is the cycle where we seek something, work towards achieving it, and when we find it, we try to hold on to it. The moment we try to hold on to it we are no longer happy because we are insecure that it may leave our hands. Again, there is conflict and after a short pause the cycle starts again.

The wise say that there is a stage in spiritual realization when the wheel stops turning. There is no more seeking, grasping or holding on. There is no fear of it being snatched away, hence there is no holding on. From the point of view of the highest spiritual experience, when the mind has become absolutely quiet, it is total and complete freedom. This is definitely accompanied by a surge of bliss and happiness that is so intense that nothing else compares to it in this world or beyond. It is an ecstasy which cannot be measured either.

Another important point is that when enlightenment really happens there is no doubt in the mind whether it is the real thing. As long as there is doubt, it is not enlightenment. Because when it happens, all boundaries are burst asunder, and there is no more doubt in the mind. In fact, that mind becomes completely different. It acts and does everything in this world like anybody else, but if you look closely there is a subtle difference in what is going on. A yogi may go and cook in the kitchen along with another person who is not enlightened, but there is a difference between the two. For instance, if hot milk falls, the reactions and responses in a yogi may be different and he may not be affected in the same way as the other person. Yes, the yogi's leg may also have a burn, but the impact is very different. There is no feeling of loss or gain in his case and no lamenting about the situation.

In the early stages of meditation, especially for those who meditate on the centres of consciousness, it begins with a peaceful and blissful feeling in the centres. When one gets absorbed in that, everything outside is forgotten at that time. But this is only temporary and hence is not enlightenment. These are only small milestones that show that there is progress. Ultimately, all doubts disappear. The whole essence of the *Ashtavakra Gita* is on this topic.

The sage Ashtavakra had eight curves or deformities in his limbs, and hence the name. He visited the great sage Janaka who was the disciple of Yajnavalkya, the great rishi of the *Brihadaranyaka Upanishad*. Janaka had mastered the art of going into samadhi at any time and experiencing profound bliss.

Ashtavakra asked Janaka if he thought he was free and, if so, why.

Janaka replied, 'Yes I am free, because I can go at will into samadhi at any time and experience it.'

Ashtavakra countered, 'What happens when you come out of samadhi?'

Janaka replied, 'When I come out of samadhi, I am not in that state anymore.'

The great sage then asked, 'If this truth is dependent on going in and coming out, then it means that it is not permanent.' He then clarified, 'It can only be called freedom if that state remains whether you are awake, dreaming or in deep sleep.'

This is only the beginning and efforts should not be neglected. Words are such an imperfect tool to express this. I have tried to explain to the extent possible.

Q: If we become still, will we feel that bliss?

M: Let's put it this way, stillness itself is bliss. We don't become anything. When we say 'bliss', we have to be very careful, because what we normally call bliss is based on our sensory experiences. When we talk about spiritual bliss, we usually assume that what we are looking for is the same happiness that we derive from sensory experiences but multiplied a hundredfold or more. Since this is what we have experienced, this is what we imagine we want.

If we can free ourselves from the complete concept and say that, 'This may be totally different, I know nothing about it', then that is the meaning of bliss from the other point of view. This means, it is not subtracted by any activity nor can any activity add to it. It is in its natural state. It's *swabhava* and this is the original swabhava— true identity. It is full in itself, nothing to be added and nothing to be taken out. This is true with everyone. It is not confined to any particular person. Everybody is entitled to it.

Q: What do you experience when you go within? Do you experience a state of 'no mind'?

M: It is something very different from what you think. Nowadays I don't go in and I don't go out. Yes, in the beginning I used to go in and experience a complete calmness of mind, and a blissful floating, an all-pervading feeling. But nowadays I neither go in nor out.

While I am talking to you, listening to you, I am still there. I am still there, my centre is still there; it's not disturbed in anyway. I may keep my eyes open. I may be talking to you, but I don't see a difference between out and in. Hence, I am no longer dependent on going in.

One is free when one need not go in or go out.

That's where I stand now. I kind of hover between going in and going out, and while I am working and doing things, there is no going out and no going in, it's the same. This is how I feel.

It's not 'no mind'. We have got this completely wrong concept that we are aiming to become thoughtless. Nobody can be thoughtless. When I say I am thoughtless, I am already there saying I am thoughtless. To be thoughtless you don't have to do sadhana, all you need is a brain haemorrhage.

All we can do to make the mind tranquil and at peace, is to be aware as a witness. You can't go beyond that. When you are there for a long time, then, very slowly, all supports move out and you are kind of neither here nor there.

In the beginning it can be quite frightening, people usually run away from it, and try to become dependent on some state which they call thoughtless, but it can't be thoughtless, because they are still aware.

Q: When people start meditating or doing kriya, how can they differentiate between an experience that is totally unrelated to the practice versus something that might be an outcome of a spiritual practice?

M: When I give kriya to somebody, I am not saying that you will get moksha because of the kriya. I'm saying that at this moment your mind is distracted, it is conflicted, it is not in proper order, and this is a technique to put the mind in a certain order. Once it's in order you will begin to see the other side.

If you have had the experience of quietness and calmness, it's because your prana has begun to operate in a certain pattern. Previously it was haphazard, but you've managed to gather it together. You may need to achieve this with kriya or something else.

You should also keep in mind that the truth is not something that can be reached through any technique. You need to practise a technique to come to a state where you have gathered all your energies together; but from there all these techniques are of no use. They are redundant when you touch *that*.

For example, right now our minds are like shapeless clay, like muck. You can't expect anything from it. If you want a beautiful statue, like this Buddha here, you need to put it in a mould. This statue was just clay once upon a time, and that clay was put into a mould to make the Buddha. But in order to see the Buddha statue, the mould had to be broken, otherwise, the Buddha would be sitting inside, and no one would be able to see it. The same is with the mind. The last step is breaking the mould, but you can't break the mould until you make the mould. So first you need the mould, the technique, to bring your mind into shape, into a state where the mind is in order, is calm and quiet.

Let me give you another example. There's a dancer who is excellent in her art and then she innovates. Now if I don't know anything about dance, can I innovate? I don't know what innovation actually means unless I have a design. It's somewhat like that.

When it comes to kriya there is not only one type. There are many types of kriya that are meant to bring your energies together instead of letting them dissipate and die. When you reach that state, of your energies coming together, when you are at optimum, there comes a time when everything falls off. Then there is nothing. The sense of agency vanishes. The mediator, the object meditated upon and the act of meditation all merge. There is nothing other than pure consciousness. All is one. There is only that mind which is free of all conflict. Free of all conditioning. Free of all memories. You will have memories like how to make tea, that's a different story. But you won't carry over all the regrets and hatred.

You can imagine how light such a brain could be. Such a brain has space. Otherwise, there is no space, it's all filled. When there is space, then the *sahasrara*, the thousand petal lotus, opens up, and instead of trying to push something up, there is something coming down, something tremendous which we cannot put into words.

Q: When you say that the prana has to rise, what do you mean by this?

M: I am referring to the ultimate energy of the universe, the whole energy that keeps the stars in place, everything, including the plants and the living beings. There is an energy, right? It is an intelligent energy. Now that energy in totality is called *parashakti*, the supreme energy. A small *amsha*, part, of that is in every human being, male or female. We see it when the sperm enters the womb into the egg and produces a complete child which can think, talk and walk. The energy after doing the work then retires and rests in one place, still complete, not having wasted anything because it is *purna*, whole.

This energy resides at the bottom of the spine in the muladhara in all living beings. Traditionally, they say it's wound three and a half times like a cobra. It's symbology, okay? There is no cobra out there. People might think, 'I was meditating, sir, and a black cobra came out.' It's a symbol of the energy coiled up. You know how the snake sleeps? If you poke it then what happens? It raises its hood and *hissssss*.

I'm deliberately not using the word kundalini. Kundalini has become a very cheap word. The other day I read in a magazine that you pay Rs 6000 and your kundalini is immediately aroused, taken to the sahasrara chakra, you're finished, you're done. Hence, I'm not using that word because it has been bandied about too much. But I'm talking about the kundalini, the prana. That prana is called *mukhya prana*, which means the most important prana, because among all the *pranic* energies it is the most important.

This mukhya prana which resides in us is usually asleep, which means it is potential energy, not kinetic. The practice of kriya and many other kinds of yoga is to awaken it and lead it through the sushumna. As you go up, your awareness moves from the gross, to the subtle, and subtle, and subtle, until you become a multidimensional being. You may be anchored on this earth, but your mind can go endlessly into different dimensions. This is what I mean by prana.

It reminds me, there's a nice drink among the Konkani Saraswats called *solkadhi*. When you say 'soul' it means the individual part of that universal consciousness which is in us. The kundalini is different from that, except when it awakens, the human mind becomes subtle and fine. When that happens, then one understands that prana, which built this whole universe, is also this prana which is within us.

Q: When I meditate, my thoughts increase—is that normal?

M: Increase? For me, they don't. I understand.

What happens is when you try to make the mind quiet, it tends to become loud. That is the mind's reaction saying, 'This fellow is going to kill me, let me stay awake, let me get up and move.'

In response, you have to watch that, and say, 'Shut up! I'm going to sit and meditate!'

There is no other way. The mind always reacts to this. When you want to sit quietly, it moves. It takes time. *Abhyasa*, practise, is very important. Keep on meditating.

Furthermore, we are engaged in so many activities, most of which are not involved in meditation or spiritual practice. It is important that we keep some activities in daily life which are conducive to your meditation. At least a few activities. This is why people do pooja, which is also an activity, but it is an activity that is conducive to spiritual practice. Today, we don't have any such activity. We only have activities that are not connected in any way with this. Therefore, it is natural that when we sit, thoughts come into our mind.

In that way, Islam has prescribed prayer five times a day. It is very good because while you are working, suddenly you stop and do your prayer, that way there is some connecting link throughout the day.

In the ancient times, they practised meditation at dawn, midday and dusk. These were called the auspicious *sandhya*s. In the midst of all your activities you had to stop your work, do the sandhya and go back to work.

Of course, when you begin, beginners in meditation are always challenged with thoughts that come up and disturb them, but you have to learn to settle them. When the thoughts come, engage them in activities which are conducive to meditation.

Q: You said that there is a possibility that we may fall asleep when in meditation, but how do we know if we are asleep or in samadhi?

M: You are saying that when you meditate you go into a state in which you can't distinguish between whether you are in meditation or asleep.

The criteria through which you differentiate between meditation and sleep is that when you go to sleep and you wake up, you will be the same person that you were before, but if you go into a spiritual state, which is called samadhi, and come back, you will be a different person. Your attitude and everything else will change as a result of the meditation.

How do you do that? You have to be alert, to not let yourself fall asleep. There are no shortcuts. I used to fall asleep when I tried to meditate as well. The mind would go calm and then I would say 'let me lie down and meditate' and that was the end of it. So don't succumb to that temptation. Sit down and meditate. And if you're really sleepy, get up, walk, wash your face with cold water and come back again. There is no other way. Keep trying until you reach the goal.

So, you distinguish between meditation and sleep based on the effects. If you are sleeping deeply, your body will be relaxed, which is good, but you will not be wiser than you were before you went to sleep. When you are in samadhi, a higher spiritual state, or whatever you want to call it, then you will find that when you wake up, something has changed.

I'm reiterating this because in the beginning, the higher spiritual state appears similar to deep sleep for some people. The reason is that the mind has not been purified enough. So the sign you have to watch out for is, 'Have I changed after this?'

This will be achieved by daily practice. There is no way out. There are no shortcuts. If anybody is offering you a short cut, especially for a sum of money, run far away. Are the poor guys who are working hard to attain it fools? Is there a shortcut through which you can reach there? No! There is no shortcut. *Nairantarya abhyasena*. Regular practice.

5

NATURE OF THE MIND AND
HOW TO CALM IT

Q: Could you please tell us something about the nature of the mind? How do we go beyond it?

M: This is a very important question and worthy of a deep discussion. I could write an entire book on this question.

What is the mind?

At this moment, I won't go into what books say about the mind. I prefer to go by how it appears to us in this current moment.

Let us start with what we know about the mind. The Sanskrit word for mind is *manas* or *mana*. Manas or mana are generic words used to describe a vast series of phenomena which portray the complex processes of thought and include many layers.

Let us look at thought as the first layer. We cannot think of a mind without thought. In fact, we cannot think at all. The moment we think, there is thought, and that can be called the mind. Hence, when we say mind, we refer to a collection of thoughts. These thoughts include not only what is in the mind at present, but also memories, which are the thoughts of yesterday and the thoughts of last year. So, the thoughts in our mind include memory.

Memories may be of pleasant experiences and painful ones. Memories include knowledge gathered from what others have said, from books, our preferences, ideas of right and wrong; memories are gathered from the time we are born until the present. While we may not distinctly remember these experiences, impressions may remain in the subconscious mind. All these are part of the memory.

The next layer involves impressions going back to what was before the womb. While I will not go into that right now, one way to look at it is from the point of evolution of the genes, a result of millions of years of evolution. We carry genetic traits from unicellular organisms, which evolved and became more complex until they became human beings.

When these genetic traits, mental impressions and thoughts come together, they form what is called mana or the mind.

The next question is, where is the mind located? When we say 'mind', we are often referring to the brain, because all thoughts of the past or the present are stored in the brain. Hence the mind includes the brain.

The reason we know the mind includes the brain is that if we starve the brain of nutrition or oxygen, we cannot think. According to the Sankhya philosophy, the subtlest part of the food we eat goes into forming the mind, which means that the mind has a physical origin and it is considered to be matter. Additional proof that the brain is part of the mind is that when certain parts of the brain are injured in an accident, certain memories disappear.

One amazing thing about the brain is that it's the centre responsible for our experience of pleasure and pain. However, on its own the brain does not experience pain. Any neurosurgeon can tell you that during neurosurgery, pain is a result of piercing the skin, bone and soft tissue surrounding the brain. But once you reach the actual brain, you can do anything without anaesthesia. The brain has no pain receptors, so there is no sensation of pain, even though it is that which controls all sensations of pain and pleasure in the body.

For the purposes of this discussion, we can conclude that thought is basically the mind—a bundle of thoughts about the past, the present and projecting into the future.

Now for the next part of your question—can we go beyond the mind?

Let's be clear, we cannot live without the mind. All imagination that has brought about this civilization is from the activities of the mind. Hence, holding the belief that we should rid ourselves of the mind is a wrong concept.

It is comical when we say we are trying to get rid of the mind because it is the mind talking about doing itself away, from itself. An impossible task! It's all one brain and one mind! One part of the mind observes and says that it doesn't like what it finds, it separates it into two and says, 'I am pure and good' and 'there is this part of me which is bad' and 'I have to control *it*'. Therefore, the one who is observing the mind is the mind itself. It is the same mind dividing itself into the observer and the observed when there is no actual difference between the two. It is the same.

When I say I am a product of all my experiences, of the pain, pleasure and sorrow I have been through, of my likes and dislikes, of ideas derived from reading and from other people, this whole package I describe is 'I' or 'me'. Now the question is, can I segregate from all this? This is the conundrum.

The Bhagavad Gita says that the mind is your friend and the mind is also your enemy. If you can make it your friend, then that mind which is destructive, becomes creative. The whole world and the imagination which has brought about the world, is from the mind. It's a great and wonderful thing. So, we should be free from the idea that the mind is a terrible thing that we should be rid of.

The question of whether we should 'go beyond the mind' is only asked when we are uncomfortable with our minds, when we see that it is not what we want it to be. But who must go beyond it? One answer may be that 'it is not me, but the atman'. But right now, that atman is also a construct of the mind, it's all a thought. There's nothing really.

However, if we can bring about order in our mind, improve the positive aspects, and not allow the negative and destructive aspects to raise their heads, then the mind is a beautiful thing. It's a beautiful tool that clears the path. But this must be cultivated. There is no other way.

The wise rishis have said, and the Upanishads have proclaimed, that there is something beyond the ordinary mind.

Now, when we hear this statement, we can only imagine that there is something beyond, because we haven't actually gone beyond it. For now, this idea is just in our mind. So how do we go beyond?

The next step is to try and find out the limitations of the mind, the limits beyond which it cannot grow or expand. To see that the mind is imperfect even when expanded to the fullest, and that it can still break, as it is merely an edifice that we have built up.

When we understand the limitations of the mind, we realize that the mind by itself cannot do anything about going beyond itself! At this stage we fall silent. This means we are not restless, there is no conflict, no fighting against anything, we are silent. In this silence we ask, 'Maybe there is a possibility of something happening which is other than the mind?' This is something that cannot be theoretically conceived, it can only be experienced.

Let's take another scenario. We just saw that the mind is the brain with memories, thoughts and impressions. But there may be a possibility that, in an average human being, there are some parts of the brain that are overly active and other parts that are not really utilized. There may be parts that are defunct and not functioning as they have never been used. Here, the question arises, are there parts of the brain which are not known to us? Is there some part of the brain which is either neglected, under-utilized, and therefore defunct? And is there a centre or some centres of the brain that can help us go beyond what we call ordinary thinking?

Great rishis and people who have experienced *it*, have said that there are certain times when certain experiences are not related to the ordinary mind. What they mean is that it happens when the mind is absolutely silent and quiet.

This cannot be done by force. If the mind is forced to be silent and is always dependent upon force to keep it still, it will definitely rebel and break out at some point. But the mind can be silenced when we are absorbed in something that is deeply interesting, or when we are totally involved in an activity which is not for the self and there is no other profit.

The mind may also be silenced when we suddenly come across a beautiful full moon rising from the clouds or the cool breeze blowing over the river. There is no profit that can come about from this, the mind is not calculating, 'Can I sell this moon? Or can I take this river home, and put it in my bank account?' When we are quiet, watching and there is a beautiful breeze blowing, you say, 'Ah! This is wonderful.'

Although these experiences occur in the mind, it is in the deepest layers of the mind. Hence, I am referring to those parts of the brain that are normally dysfunctional but are now activated, not through force, but because the mind has fallen silent, where it's not looking for an escape but is just quiet.

In that tranquility, a new dimension opens, and it leads to that which is beyond the mind. This can also happen when there is a very deep emotion and you cannot think. But we are afraid of that. We are frightened because we think that the mind will collapse if the mind goes, 'How am I going to exist?' Therefore, we successfully avoid it by either comparing it with something else or trying to bring in a substitute thought. We don't allow ourselves to be in that black hole which is the beginning of all creation, because we fear losing our personal identity.

Q: Can you please explain the statement in the Bhagavad Gita, 'the mind can be your friend and it can be your enemy too'?

M: Your mind can be your friend and your mind can be your enemy. This is a well-known fact. If you keep your mind trained and creative, channel it for doing good things, then it's your friend. If you allow it to go berserk and do whatever it wants to do, then naturally it will turn into an enemy. To say that the mind is a friend and the mind is an enemy, means we already have an understanding of what the mind is.

When we say the mind is a friend and the mind is an enemy, we are only talking about how it manifests itself, either as a friend or as an enemy. We are not talking about the mind as such, but how it operates in day-to-day life.

It is important to trace the root of the word 'mind' and find out when we say mind, what do we mean by it. Unfortunately, in English there is only one word—mind—in which many things are included. In Sanskrit, there are many words for the mind, there is *buddhi*, there is manas, there is *ahankara*, showing different aspects of the mind.

When we think of consciousness, we also call it the mind. The moment we say mind, it means thought because we cannot conceive of a mind without thought. Therefore, the mind as we know it, is a collection of thoughts from the past, touching the present and moving into the future. This is the mind.

Next comes the question of language. If you look carefully, we always think in a language. You cannot think without a language. The moment you try to think, there is already a language at work saying the words. It may depend on the background we are brought up in, or what language we were taught in, but every mind thinks in a language, which is why language has become so important. Since we think in a language, language has incredible influence over the mind, as it can be manipulated by words.

Therefore, what we call the mind, which consists of thought expressing itself in words through a language, is what we call brain or consciousness. We can't be conscious without the mind. When we say consciousness, we refer to the phenomenon that 'I am aware', but that in itself is a thought.

All our thoughts are normally brain-based, they are formulated in a language and are necessary for our day-to-day survival. However, the big question is, can there be thought without a language? If there is a thought without a language, perhaps that thought may not be brain-based. Or perhaps it has much to do with the brain. But most of our thought is brain-based, because it is all in a language, it is structured.

So, is there thought without language?

I think the corruption of humanity started with the invention of language. When a feeling is translated into language, it always reflects the preconceived ideas in the brain of the person speaking that language.

The old Biblical story of the tower of Babel comes to mind. In fact, the word babble comes from Babel. There was once a great king called Nimrod who decided to build a tower, a palace so high that if he shot an arrow from the top, it would hit the throne of God. In those days there was only one language. If we examine the story closely, there could not have been only one language because it is said that people came from all nations to work to build the tower. It could not be only one language with people coming from so many different directions. Perhaps in those days thought was expressed through feelings in the mind.

So, Nimrod built a very tall tower and when they completed it, Nimrod went to the top. It is said he could almost hear the rumbling up in heaven. He took out his bow and arrow and shot an arrow onto the throne of God. The moment the arrow hit the throne something happened. People who came from different nations who had one tongue, suddenly found themselves speaking in different languages and were not able to understand each other. They fought and killed each other and there was complete chaos. The tower broke and fell. In man's ambition to shoot the throne of God, beautiful languages were invented all over the world, and these languages became the cause of disharmony.

This disharmony starts here in the mind, because every mind thinks in a language.

The question is, can there be thought without a language? If there is a thought where no language is involved, then perhaps that thought is not of the brain and may not be a divisive thought. We may call it consciousness or awareness.

Let's start with something ordinary, something which we know, then we can go into something subtler. Let's take the sound of someone playing the flute, or, say, Bismillah Khan Saheb who used to play the shehnai every morning in the temple before Kashi Viswanath in Varanasi. Or, we may have heard Hariprasad Chaurasia, a beautiful violin recital by Pannalal, or the great symphonies of Beethovan. This is music, there are no words.

Music has been formulated in symbols. Now pure music cuts across boundaries, languages and across all divisions, everyone enjoys it! It has no language. While listening to it, the mind functions in a non-language mode.

This layer of the mind is closer to the source, that which is not part of the brain. Neurologists may argue that the brain listens to music even though music itself has no language. Therefore, it is possible that music may be close to thought, but without a language.

All disciplines that are connected to going within the deeper layers of one's mind and touching that part of consciousness which is not part of a language, are not divisive.

This includes the sound of music, pure music without language. I frequently enjoy Hindustani music by great masters, mainly because I cannot understand a single word they are saying. Usually there's only one sentence, you can only hear the *aalaap*. Of course, when I listen to a song with good lyrics, I enjoy it, but then there is association, again there is language.

Deep feelings are another example of that which is beyond language and still a part of the mind. While deep feelings may manifest through language, you don't actually need a language.

Music, art, abstractions, feelings, these are things that don't require definitions, which do not have structural components, these are closer to the inner aspects of the mind. They are closer to the root of the essence of our consciousness, which perhaps may not have much to do with the brain, except when manifested. Perhaps this is the root of thought, and it is non-divisive. The moment language steps in, it is divisive.

Language unites and divides. While it has functions in unity, it also has divisive functions. Often the language we are born into or are familiar with seems wonderful, while others do not. It may not be obvious, but it is there.

So, the mind that is a friend is a mind without divisive qualities and attributes. The other mind, which is the enemy, has seeds of divisiveness in it. Therefore, the mind which is not divisive, which is the friend, is the mind that has nothing to do with language. It has more to do with feelings and with music. This is why bhakti and bhava, devotion and feeling, are important. Even the study of Vedantic texts, with great understanding and intellectual acumen, is within the boundary of a language. But when we allow ourselves to go into feeling, into bhava, we are out of this framework. It is all one. I am talking about music—pure, melodious music.

When I say feelings, I mean deep feelings, feelings that cannot be expressed in words. When we see something extraordinary, we say there are no words to describe it. This demonstrates that words have a limited function, they have a point beyond which they cannot express, however much we polish them. Hence, *that* which no words can describe and where the mind of thought and language cannot reach, is that which is the source and essence of all beings. The *Keno Upanishad* says, '*Yan manasanamanyute*', which translates to 'That which even the mind cannot reach'.

Now we need to be careful, it does not mean that if the mind cannot reach, we don't need to do anything about it. What it means is that the mind, which is only caught up in the region of language, definitions, limitations and divisiveness, cannot reach that. The mind actually falls silent when it understands this fact. When that happens then it may be possible to go into the deeper layers of one's consciousness. Then the mind is a friend. It is no more an enemy. It is also a fact that it cannot be touched as long as the mind is within the boundaries of so-called spoken language.

This is why a few who have touched it cannot say anything when they come back, because no words can express it.

Ramakrishna Paramahamsa had many notable disciples, both monks and householders, but there was one person who cannot in any way be compared to any of the stalwarts of the order. While there were many sincere seekers, there were people who would meditate for hours together, there was one person called Girish Chandra Ghosh, who was a famous dramatist, a stage artist, poet, playwright and producer of plays in Kolkata.

Girish Chandra Ghosh had every known vice on earth. He could be found in different houses at different times in all areas, red, blue, yellow, whatever. He was an alcoholic; from morning to evening he would be under the influence of the other spirit. But he was very fond of Ramakrishna. There was a bond between them which nobody could understand. He would come, sit with him, talk to him, and sometimes abuse him. He used to come late at night after finishing all his activities, get drunk and abuse the Master. Many people told Sri Ramakrishna, 'Why are you entertaining this man, who is a drunk and always abusing you? You just have to say the word and we will throw him out.' And Ramakrishna used to say, 'This is between him and me, you need not interfere.'

This is how real Masters are. Ramakrishna did not ask him to be thrown out because he knew that deep down in this man there was a spark, which if ignited, could become a blazing fire. So he kept him close. Girish Chandra tried hard but he could not change his way of life, but he was sure that he had to find *that* something in him, and he loved the Master.

One day, he came to the Master and said, 'What am I to do, so many people have come to you and become great yogis, holy men, but look at me, I am still like this, why don't you do something?'

Ramakrishna said, 'Can you give me your power of attorney?'

Girish responded quickly, 'Yes.'

The Master said, 'Wait a minute, you are going to run into trouble, so think carefully. When you give me your power of attorney, it has to be unconditional.'

Girish said, 'Yes, this is unconditional.'

When he went back after this episode, he could not drink again because when he took the glass he could only see the Master's smiling face in it. Later on, when Swami Vivekananda came back from the West, he introduced many of his Western disciples to Girish Chandra Ghosh, saying, 'Here is a man who's a miracle in spiritual life, it is one of the Master's miracles that he is a man of stature today.'

Q: You have said that we should not stick to thoughts that are entertaining. What did you mean by that?

M: There's nothing wrong with entertaining thoughts. The human mind sometimes needs entertainment, as it cannot be in a state of constant flux and stress.

What I said was that if you are searching for the truth, then on the way you may need to drop what is entertaining. We may think that something is the truth because it is very convenient and enjoyable. We may actually conclude that we are established in truth, that we know it.

Let's take an example. If we have a headache, we may need to take a tablet to get rid of it. We know that the tablet may not be a solution for the headache, but we may take it for immediate relief to be free of the pain. Karl Marx said, 'Religion is an opiate of the masses.' People take this comment to be a criticism, but I think it is constructive.

Only when we are free of the headache, can we think clearly. When we are suffering, we cannot think, so it takes some opiate to be free of that pain or stress. Once the pain is no longer there, we don't stick to the medicine, we throw it away and think for ourselves.

Entertainment is the same. Sometimes it can be essential. We meet friends, go for walks, eat good food, all this is part of entertainment, and it does not work without that for human beings. Hence, some entertainment is essential, but don't mistake entertainment for the actual thing.

People say that they are free of all rituals, but then end up creating their own. New rituals come up when human society, which is the human mind living in society, creates its own rituals. Some rituals are essential perhaps for the well-being of an individual, but not for a person who is free. He or she who is truly free needs no rituals. But one need not imitate that.

While entertainment is essential for our well-being and our sanity, it is not actually the truth! So, while we are still with a clear mind, try to find what we are looking for, otherwise we get bogged down by the entertainment and do not move forward to the actual.

How do we do this? We need to watch thoughts carefully, especially the ones that give us a feeling of well-being, or the ones we are too comfortable with. Examine them with attention. We need to watch our minds carefully and figure it out for ourselves.

There are very few people who are really searching for the truth. Generally, people seek for their own convenience. Very few people seek only the truth. People are either in search of entertainment, spiritual entertainment, or their version of the truth which may be convenient and wonderful for them.

Another reason is the seeking for a feeling of security. The moment they realize that the truth may be something which does not guarantee security, they don't want to search for this. There is nothing to hang on to, everything is pulled from under your feet! This is a very serious affair. Do we really want to search?

Q: My mind chatters so much. Why is the nature of the mind to chatter? Why are we all not established in silence? And rather have the mind come in only when we use it, like other muscles?

M: Why is it the nature of the mind to chatter? I don't know the 'why', but I can tell you that it chatters.

You see, sometimes we ask a question in order to find out 'why so-and-so happens', because we don't want to face the fact that it is happening.

I don't know why, you don't know why, and while somebody in a book might give you an answer as to why the mind chatters, it is in the book and is only an idea. The reality is that nobody actually knows 'why' it chatters. However, we know that it does, and since we know that it does, the question is, can we get out of it?

Can 'I' get out of it? 'I' cannot get out of it, because 'I' am the one chattering.

Do you note this? It is 'I', who is part of the chattering. How can 'I' get out of it? 'I' cannot. So when I say 'I cannot', then what happens? This is a little tricky, so let me try and give you an example. Suppose I am sitting here under this tree, and I say, 'I want to get out of this chattering', but I know 'I' can't get out of this chattering because 'I' am the one that is chattering. Who is trying to run away from chattering? It is 'I' who is chattering. Is this possible? No. I find that there is no escape, so I just sit under the tree and make no attempt whatsoever. No going in, no going out. Let go and rejoice.

See, when I say 'the mind is chattering and I want to stop it', the chattering increases because I want to stop it. Now there are two voices, one who is chattering, and another who is trying to stop the chatter. But actually there is only one, which is the chatter which is my mind.

What happens is that we are accustomed to splitting our minds into two. One part says 'I am very pure', and by 'one part' I mean 'one part of the mind', because without thought you cannot say this. So one part of my mind says 'I am very pure' and being pure is good. What I meant is, one part says 'I am very pure' and then it says 'but there is this other part of me that is very bad'. Again, this is a thought, a part of the mind. All these thoughts are from the same mind, we are the ones that are making the division and saying 'this is bad because it is angry', 'this is bad because it is jealous', and 'I am something very pure', 'so now I have to control it', 'I have to escape it', etc. This splitting of the mind, splitting of any kind, is conflict.

Hence, can we say, 'it's all one'? Can we say that there is no escape, and sit quietly? The moment you look for escapes you are chattering again.

Are you able to follow? Sometime it's very difficult to explain, not because it is complicated, but because we have many ideas in our head, otherwise it is very simple.

Are there two minds within us or only one? And what is it made of? Thought. One part of the mind is saying 'I have to be thoughtless', while the other part is always thinking. In actuality, the thinking one is the same as the thoughtless one, there is no difference. If you get over the difference and see only one that is called *advaita*. Advaita is not the mind saying, 'I am the Brahman and the world is an illusion.' That is rubbish. The world is not an illusion. How long can you stay without eating if the world is an illusion?

It is this 'split' that is the illusion. If you hit upon that silence, then there is no split and the mind stops chattering. But don't ask me 'how' you hit upon that silence. If I say 'how', then it becomes a method, and I don't know that there is any method for that. The understanding is more important. Suppose I find that silence, then it is everywhere, it is here, it is there. When you sit down on the grass . . . everywhere!

Actually, I am not doing the right thing, because by sitting on the grass, the grass is crying. It doesn't cry like a baby, you can't hear it, but it is crying because we are sitting down and pressing it. We can't help it, that's a different matter. We are not saints. We also have problems. But when we understand these things, then everything lives and becomes one. There is no difference. Why? Because there is only one mind, from which thoughts come like waves in the ocean, and if the waves become still, there is only the ocean.

Let's look at this question in a different way.

The mind is always asking for something, or it is running away from something. These are the two major factors. Either it is attached to something or it is repelled by something. If these two factors are present, then the chattering will never stop. So can we try to be without too much attachment and too much repulsion? Because if these two things are there, there cannot be quietness of mind. Can we be free of this? I think it is possible.

When we sit quietly in solitude, can we just sit, doing nothing whatsoever? If we can, then silence slowly comes in. But don't be in a hurry. And when that silence comes, it remains with you. It remains even in the marketplace, and you can sit in the marketplace and be absolutely silent, despite all the noise that is around you, because your mind has stopped chattering. That's the joy.

The problem is not the sound of the bus, or the helicopter, or the plane. The problem is your mind, my mind, our mind, that mind which has not stopped chattering.

Can we consider that there may be a part of the mind which is not chattering? Give it a thought. When we sit quietly, can we sit without saying, 'Yes this, not this, this, not this'? Can we sit without the two opposites in our mind?

I think it is possible. In the depths of your heart there is a silence, a silence which you sometimes come upon when you look suddenly at a lake or at a mountain.

I think the reason why we don't come upon it is because we compare and judge. We compare and we judge. For example, I am standing on the terrace of my house and I see the full moon. Great, for some time everything is frozen and there is no chattering, there is nothing. I am looking at the moon and then out of nowhere, comes the chattering mind. I say, 'Ah, in 1958 I saw another moon, which was like a crescent, it was peeping.' The moon that is in front of me is completely gone from my sight, I've stopped seeing it and instead the chattering has begun. Then I begin to compare, 'The other day there was this moon, and that's the day my wife threw a spoon at me, and then . . .' You know how the mind works? No, my wife didn't actually throw a spoon at me, I am just joking.

Instead of this comparison, can we look at somebody and simply say 'she is good'? And not say 'somebody is like this, somebody is like that'? If I cease to compare, then I see goodness. The moment I compare, I am in trouble. Can we look at things without comparing? Without saying 'oh he is better', 'she is better', 'I am so bad', 'I am so superior', 'that person is so bad'. Can we do that? Because we all are a part of this mind.

If we stop this comparison, then the mind has no choice but to stop chattering.

Q: You said we can understand our nature when we are interacting with others. But you have also said that periods of isolation are very good for understanding the mind.

M: Let's replace the word isolation with solitude. There is a difference in these two words. Isolation may mean a forced separation which is usually not voluntary. It may involve others isolating you. Solitude means trying to seek a place where you are quiet.

Solitude is necessary because after a period of intense activity in this world you want to think carefully and introspect, it is required. It is not because you are pushed out. For example, busy executives work through the year and then go on a holiday. Why? To be free of the mental and physical routine and free up the mind for a while. Only then can one think of more serious matters. So, introspection is very important when you are in solitude, and solitude is essential.

Solitude doesn't necessarily mean that we should go and sit in a cave. It means any place where one can sit quietly, without the regular routine daily disturbances of the cook, watchman or anybody else, and do nothing that will tax one's energies too much. It does not mean one sleeps all the time. That is easy to do!

Look for a quiet place where you can go for long walks, observe the plants, look at the trees, the rivers, sit down and quietly close your eyes and go within and see how the mind is. What is this mind? How is it travelling? Am I the root cause of all this? How do I extricate myself from this? This is called solitude. And it is essential. This is not to say solitude is futile while there is no communication with the world. It's only when we have six months of communication with the world that one can begin to feel the difference when one comes to a place of solitude. Otherwise the difference is not felt.

Happiness, what we normally call happiness, is a small interval between two sorrows. One sorrow has vanished, and the other has not yet appeared, so we are happy for some time. When one observes the mind, we see that today I desire something, and I work for it, I acquire it, and this makes me happy for a while as I am no longer putting in effort to get it. I experience a state of effortlessness, but as soon I am dissatisfied with it, I look for something else. It is only an interim period before there is agitation, movement and activity. Then I acquire the next thing and again there is temporary satisfaction. When we observe the mind, we see that this satisfaction actually is the mind.

There is a sense of attainment because I have acquired something and that peace lasts for a while. There is happiness. Something else sets in that we are not happy with. Again, we move towards another thing and on achieving it, we are happy. Why? Because the mind is at rest. When something is acquired, the mind is at rest; when it is in the act of acquiring, it is not at rest.

What if there were a way to always keep the mind at peace, irrespective of whether you are acquiring or not? Is this the root of happiness? If this truth is really understood, not just theoretically, then it is possible to bring about that change in the mind without any effort or doing anything.

Q: Should a married couple go to solitude together or separately?

M: I don't know, that is for you to decide. If you do, if you can be together and still be in solitude, great! If you want to separate, it's up to you, but then both people should understand that 'We are not against each other but we want some solitude.' Right, so it's not a bad idea to have some solitude.

Q: Is introspection an important aspect in understanding the mind?

M: Introspection is the most important part. In Shankaracharya's *Vivekachudamani*, both *vichara* and *viveka*, are considered to be very important parts of understanding life. The word 'introspect' means to look carefully at all that is happening in oneself, to look at our interactions with the world. It is not to look for anything in particular.

To introspect is to examine the relationship between you and I, the world and I. How do I react in different situations? If there is a reaction, why do I react this way? This is called introspection. This happens along with watching the mind carefully, watching how it gets caught up by various desires or how it cannot do without a certain thing because the mind gets so habituated to something that it cannot leave it.

Introspection also means, 'Am I seriously looking for freedom from all of this? Or am I only looking at a minor, cosmetic alteration of my being? Am I happy with a couple of "feel-good" medicines and placebos? Or am I trying to find the root cause of the disease? Am I ready to bring in drastic changes that may be required for a total cure?'

Q: Is meditation the only answer to calm the mind or is there anything else one can do?

M: Meditation is not the only answer. While meditation is a good technique, the answer is to fix your attention on things which are linked to your spiritual practice. For example, if you have a background of worshipping a certain deity in your family for many years, whom you consider to be a manifestation or representation of God, then sit down and try to do that, so that your mind effortlessly travels to it.

The reason why there is distraction of the mind is because we don't like many of the things we do. I am forcing myself to meditate. I don't want to meditate. But I am forcing myself. Suppose that deep down, I really want to meditate, then when I meditate, there is no distraction. Suppose you love music, if you love music, do you get distracted when you are listening to this music? No.

Hence, apart from doing the meditation practice, listen to beautiful music that will take your mind and somewhat quell the restlessness. But it should be good music. Singing is also good. In fact, if you sing and you are completely absorbed in it, that is a great meditation by itself.

Don't confine meditation to a technique. Meditation is to be fully absorbed in something with the exclusion of something else. This is meditation. Choose what appeals to you, but don't say the other is wrong.

I think since you are interested in music, listening and singing, you should concentrate on something that takes you into the musical journey. Play an instrument, listen to an instrument, or listen to songs and let your mind be fully absorbed. Then there is no distraction. And if it continues for some time, your mind will learn how to stay without distractions. If you think there is some technique which might help you, then practise it.

Q: Do you have advice on 'positive thinking'? My family often says I look at the glass half-empty and that I need to be more positive.

M: You know, I personally don't have anything against empty. Empty is great. We have associated emptiness with something terrible. So if a glass is half-empty, it's nice. If it's not empty, how will you fill it? Emptiness has been given a bad name. It's not like that.

When people say a glass is half-full or half-empty, they are talking about people who are always negative, only look at the negative side and do not look at the positive side. That's why people say, 'Oh look, the glass is half-full.' But the reality is that because the glass is half-full, it is also half-empty. There is no actual dichotomy between the two.

Wherever there is emptiness, it is filled. Why is something filled? Because there is emptiness. So I think emptiness is a wonderful thing. Always think emptiness is a great thing.

The Buddhists say the ultimate nirvana is shunya. What is shunya? Zero. So, I think your husband must be a positive thinker, but I think you are not negative either in daily life.

People always have an association that empty must mean darkness. But darkness is beautiful. In fact, the word used in Sanskrit for dark is *krishna*. Krishna was dark. In Sanskrit, white is *shukla*, dark is krishna. So, let's not draw this line dividing things into black and white. There are many grey areas in this world.

This system of something being 'absolutely evil' or 'absolutely good', like Satan and God, is a very Semitic idea. In ancient Indian teachings, there are asuras and devas but the Supreme Being is beyond both. Furthermore, there are some good asuras, and there are some bad devas. What do you do?

There is no line which separates this into two watertight compartments. Somebody may be good and bad and good, it's all a mixture. You know what I mean?

Q: It is said that 80 per cent of the brain is not being used. How do we go about using this?

M: First let us speculate that there are other regions of the brain that need to be explored. Let's look at the science of yoga. Every chapter of the Bhagavad Gita has been called yoga—'Arjuna Visaada Yoga', 'Sankhya Yoga', etc. According to these, to the science of yoga, there are different approaches that have been prescribed to tap the centres of the mind and system.

In this, we start with trying to control the autonomic nervous system through centres which are called the plexuses. You will see that there are plexuses where the chakras are marked. If you want a simple practice to tap into the mind, start by just sitting down and watching your breath.

There is no other initiation. This is initiation. To initiate means to begin something, to put somebody on the track. No dark rooms and mysteries! If it looks very mysterious then shun it. Truth is like the sun. It falls on every human being and others as well.

Q: What is the nature of the mind of a spiritually established person?

M: The Bhagavad Gita calls a spiritually balanced person a *sthitapragna*. This means one whose mind has become still, quiet and tranquil, and one who, under all circumstances, remains steady. This is because such a person has delved deep into his own inner self and discovered a spark of consciousness in us all—you may call it atman or the self. This is our true identity that cannot be disturbed, shaken, broken or killed.

When one is definitely established in this knowledge, not just theory, but as a true, personal, lived experience, only then does such a person becomes a sthitapragna.

A person like this is not necessarily confined to a small room, meditating all the time. He might be in the marketplace, in the hub of all activity, but in the midst of all this, he remains calm. That is the criteria. A person who remains calm in all circumstances, even if all activity is taken away from him by force, he's still calm, inside there is absolute silence.

Now it may be necessary for him sometimes to act as if he is disturbed while functioning in the world, but he won't really be affected by these matters. It is possible for only a yogi to live like that.

People often ask me, if you live like that all the time, and people realize that nothing disturbs you and that you do not cause harm to others, won't they try to create problems for you? How do you handle this?

First, for any person who has touched the inner core, there is automatically an intelligence operating which knows how to deal with these matters in the best possible way. Second, one sometimes may have to put on an act, but deep down there is no feeling of abuse or hatred, so this is not a problem. We are all living in this world, we are not living in a cave far away from society.

Let me tell you a story about the brahmachari and the snake. Let's suspend our disbelief for a while, because in this story, the snake talks.

There once was a snake, a very dangerous and poisonous one, living in a hole in a village. Nobody would walk along that street because of this dangerous snake. It would attack and kill people unprovoked. One day, a brahmachari came and wanted to walk down the street where the snake lived. The boys from the village said, 'Please be careful, you may not be alive once you go there as there is this cobra which can attack anybody.' But the brahmachari said he could handle it and went down the street.

The story goes that when the snake came to bite him, he chanted a mantra and the snake became peaceful. When the snake discovered this peace, he asked the brahmachari to grant him this peace permanently and asked what steps it could take towards this. The brahmachari gave him advice and a condition. The condition was that the snake should not bite anybody from then on. 'No biting,' said the brahmachari. The snake, like a true disciple, agreed to this condition and went back into its hole.

After a year, the brahmachari came back to the village. To his surprise, he found that everybody was walking along the street where the snake lived, children were playing marbles and so on. He asked the children where the snake had gone. They replied, 'Oh! That fellow, he's inside the hole, he's broken his back.' The brahmachari went to the hole to check and see how the snake was doing, wondering if it was alive!

The brahmachari, the snake's Guru, peeped into the hole and found the snake lying there. He called out to him and when the snake appeared, crawling slowly and painfully, the guru asked him what had happened.

The snake was very happy to see him and said, 'Oh! Guruji, you have come, wonderful, I am practising exactly what you said. My mind is very peaceful. All that is true. But I can't move easily now. When the children found out that I don't bite anymore, they stoned me and broke my backbone.'

The guru, as all gurus do, is said to have pulled him out and cured his back. After this, he said, 'You fool, I told you not to bite, I didn't ask you not to hiss.'

Sometimes, in this world, we may have to hiss, but never bite. While we may do this sometimes, we also have to ensure that it doesn't affect our inner self. The challenge is that human beings are very intelligent, there is no way to fool them, as soon enough they discover that there is only hissing but no sting, then one must handle it carefully. It is true however that there is an inner intelligence that works for us and helps us handle these things.

We may sometimes get into situations where we don't know what to do. So how do we handle it? We go back to the inner source and then from that core, comes a calmness which spreads to our whole being. When that happens, the other person who has been creating trouble for us slowly imbibes a bit of it and receives peace. So it is resolved. This is how things work.

Q: You said that all the problems, the whole problem, is with the mind. This mind, that mind, all minds. But is the mind not a part of the subtle, ever-present consciousness? This is my idea of it.

M: That is your idea of it, right? Hence, it is still in the mind. The problem is with the mind.

Q: But how can we get rid of this problem?

M: You cannot get rid of it. You have to accept it. You have to accept it with the feeling that, 'It must not be there', but in order to do that, first you have to see it. The problem is we try to get rid of it quickly. This is as good as sweeping dust under the carpet and hiding it. You should see it, fully, and when you see it fully, it is gone. You don't need to do anything.

Q: Even if I see it fully . . .

M: You are not seeing it fully, that is the problem.

Q: But even if we look . . .

M: But you are not looking properly, you are looking at it with the idea that 'there is one consciousness'. Get rid of all these thoughts and see it as it is.

6

OBSTACLES IN MEDITATION

Q: I don't enjoy meditation, I get bored very quickly. Is there something else I can do instead of meditation?

M: If you are serious about meditation I don't think you will be bored with meditation. That is very strange. Perhaps you are not really interested in it. Perhaps you are doing it because someone is asking you to. Perhaps your goals are not clear, you don't know what you want and you're just doing it because 'everybody is doing it'. Therefore, 'I'm bored when I'm meditating.' We'll find out why.

If you feel that 'when I sit down to meditate I'm bored', then you shouldn't be meditating, you should be doing something else. Go for a walk, cut firewood, do something that keeps you occupied so that you don't get bored. You can read if you like. If you are still interested in meditation, then read things which talk about meditation so that it will provide an inducement for it. That's a good thing to do.

There are several ways you can occupy yourself if you can't meditate and you are bored. You can do some gardening, go near flowers and smell them, watch birds, you can do several things and never get bored. For example, if you look out the window, every minute the scene is changing. One bird is coming, another is going, one is hovering above like a plane at Frankfurt airport waiting to descend. The other one is still, as if on the tarmac. You don't get bored.

Once, a young man came from Kerala with a friend of mine to Vasant Vihar in Chennai when I was at the Krishnamurthi Foundation. My friend told me that this young man was constantly high on grass but that he wanted to come and listen to Krishnamurthi's talks. I said it was fine. So, the man sat down and listened and was smiling ecstatically when Krishnamurthi spoke—I think he was already nicely drugged with cannabis. At the end of the talk I asked, 'How did you like it? What did you feel?' He said, 'It was very nice, but then I know all of this, he doesn't have to tell me.' So if you are very bored, you know what to do. Not that I recommend it.

Q: Sometimes when some people meditate, they frequently fall asleep. What can one do?

M: Yes. The first question is, 'Why do they fall asleep?' It means the meditation is successful, in the sense that the mind has become quiet. When the mind becomes quiet it has only two options. The first is that it goes into samadhi, which is the super-conscious state. The second option is that though the mind is relaxed, since the mind is still full of confusion and is not ready yet for that state, when it is relaxed it goes into sleep.

When you sit to meditate, if you are falling asleep it means that the meditation is working to some extent, but the channels are not clear. If this is the case, then the next step is to figure out why the channels are not clear and why you are not able to go to higher levels. Why are you falling asleep instead? The reasons for this might include being overweight, consuming improper food, insufficient sleep, or a general disinterest in what you are doing. If you look into these factors and try to sort them out, then you will not fall asleep afterwards.

However, if you say, 'I will figure that out later, but right now I want to meditate', if you still fall asleep then the best thing is to keep some ice-cold water and splash it on your face, wake up and sit up again. Or if you have confidence in the guru then say, 'Give me a tight slap.' These are practical things you can do. Not the slap, but the cold water!

In the long term, the thing to check and see is what kind of wrong foods or habits are making you sluggish. Are you overeating? Is your sleep insufficient? Or do you work so hard that you are tired? You need to work on this. A yogi is not advised to work in such a manner that he becomes very tired, he or she. He should do everything in moderation, including work. Then you can change the fact that you are falling asleep during meditation.

Q: There have been times when I meditate and times when I don't. And even when I meditate, I get distracted. What should I do?

M: Make a proper schedule and try to internalize your mind for at least fifteen to twenty minutes every day. You can easily do this by just watching your breath. Put in a little more effort.

I think what you need is perhaps a few days of solitude once every three or four months. Find a place where you can go, preferably somewhere you don't know anybody, or they don't know you, otherwise it gets complicated. Even in a spiritual place, like an ashram, if you know too many people then you get caught up in that. Go to a place absolutely alone, a beautiful place. I'm sure Australia has many lovely places. Stay there a few days and just do your meditation, chanting Om, breathe in and out, take in the fresh air, go for walks, do nothing in particular. You shouldn't even make the effort to make a cup of tea, it should be available.

I think if you do that maybe once every three to four months for ten days or a week, it would help you to deepen your meditation. I know theoretically you know many things, but it has to come from inside.

There is a lot of hope. Good hope.

Q: When I am dealing with a particularly stressful person or situation, it is very hard to empty the mind; do you let the thoughts come or try and block them?

M: It depends on the person. These are very individual things. It's difficult to empty the mind of thoughts like that, because the mind cannot stay empty. It is like nature. Nature cannot bear having a vacuum, air immediately rushes in. It's the same with the mind, if you try to keep the mind blank, more thoughts will rush in. It's normal.

Therefore, the idea is that instead of emptying the mind, engage your mind in some activity within, which is not connected to external activity. One example is the breath, where for some time the mind can be systematically connected into a pattern of following what is happening inside. Here you can be free of disturbing thoughts for a period of time, because the only thought is your breath. As you continue to keep your attention there, you progress, and one day while watching your breath you will notice that everything is fine, the stress is no longer there. Then you let go of that as well.

If you keep cutting all the thoughts separately, they keep sprouting like grass. When you go to the core, then you might one day experience that disturbance-less state.

Hence, first start by fixing your attention internally because the mind refuses to keep quiet without any action. Give it the action of the breath. Let it be completely engaged in that, like a routine. You will begin to notice that while it's there, it's calm because there is no time or no occasion for it to get caught up outside, and as you go on doing that for a long time, one day you let go of that. Not before that. When you let go, then there is something tremendous happening, which is beyond our understanding. It's not part of conditioned thought.

To attempt to reach there while your mind is still disturbed is not possible.

You need practice, and as you practise, it shouldn't be that it becomes a mere ritual. You must watch out for that. If you're doing everything, but your mind is still somewhere else, you have to bring it back again and again.

However, what happens is, when the breath becomes quiet and systematic, and everything is still, then there is something which you begin to enjoy inside. When this happens, then you are done. You don't need to worry about it.

Do you know why the mind wanders? Because it is seeking enjoyment outside. If you give it something, if you give it honey to suck, then it will come back.

Q: Sometimes when I sit down to meditate, my mind is filled with a lot of anxiety about the future or fear of the past. What do you suggest for people like me?

M: Is this only an issue when you sit down to meditate or even during normal times?

Q: Both, but more so during meditation because they become clear when I meditate.

M: So it's a good reason to meditate! Because then you are clear on what the problem is and you can sort it out. Anxiety and fear shouldn't be an excuse to avoid meditation. When you sit down to meditate, and you have these fears, you know exactly what these fears are. This gives you the opportunity to figure out these fears, so you can solve them. You should meditate more. Try to sit for more time. The mind will ruminate, go around, wander about with all this fear. Then it will get tired and settle down. Don't avoid meditation because of that.

Q: And can the same be said for other difficult emotions like anger?

M: Of course! Sometimes when you sit down to meditate, anger, which was deeply hidden somewhere within your mind, comes out. You see it face to face and you say, 'Hello, there you are.' So you are here! I'm not joking, seriously. You are able to see it. If you don't see it, then how will you sort it out?

I always like to think of anger and other emotions as little things, like birds. They come, you look at them and say, 'Hi, hello, little things', and then they fly away. When you try to actually look into them, to take a picture, they vanish. I'm telling you, it's happened! Not only with birds, but it is also true with humans. When you carefully examine the emotions that come, they become very uncomfortable, and then you'll see after some time that 'Hey, it's gone!'

Q: Wouldn't it be simpler to suppress our emotions instead of letting our emotions run around?

M: I gather that when such emotions come up, you want to get rid of them. And I'm guessing that you think the emotions are negative, which they may or may not be, but you think they are. So, you try to handle them and when you do, for the time being they disappear. But then they come back again.

When we practically live in this world, it is necessary to do that at times, but the reality is that they come back, so that's not a permanent solution. The permanent solution is to come face-to-face and look at them and try to understand why they come. If you cut the 'why', then they will not come again.

There are a couple of simple reasons as to why these emotions come up. First is, I have an ego, which when rubbed on the wrong side, reacts. Second is, when something is good, but somebody else thinks it is not good, there is a clash. Third is, I have some emotional feelings about something, but my reason doesn't agree with it.

There are many reasons for why emotions come up, and while it is necessary in this world to have a temporary solution, like sweeping them under the rug and so on, it's important to be ready to lift the rug when you want to look at it again. You want to get rid of it permanently, right?

Otherwise you can sweep it under the rug and deal with it temporarily, but it will come back. But if you are happy with the situation, then no problem.

Q: How can we be free from the pull of emotions?

M: No, you need not be free from emotion. All emotion is not bad. Some emotions are good and necessary, like the emotion of affection, that is also an emotion. The emotion of love is also good. What we should avoid is emotions of hatred, emotions of fear, emotions of wanting to cause damage to somebody else. These emotions should be avoided but other good emotions like love and affection and good thoughts and good deeds should be kept alive.

Now, the only way to avoid the negative is to increase the positive. Deliberately increase the positive so there's no place for the negative to come in. Then, your emotions are under your control. Otherwise you are under the control of your emotions.

Emotions are thoughts, in the sense that most emotions end up in thought and many thoughts begin with emotion. They are interlinked. Why? Because emotion is felt in our mind and we cannot feel anything in our mind without the process of thought. However, when emotion is raw, for a split second there is no thought. The problem is when emotion is mixed with thought; when it is pure, by itself, it is coming from the inner core of your consciousness.

For example, suppose I suddenly feel angry, now anger doesn't wait for us, right? It just comes. Through practice, it is possible to catch the moment when the anger arises, but one has to be very careful and observant to do this. If you practise it as a meditation technique, saying every time I get angry, I am going to be very, very aware of it, then when the anger comes in a rush, if you are aware of it, it will not translate into action. Instead it will stay inside you as an emotion and if you allow yourself to fully feel it, you will find the emotion of anger is no different from the emotion of love, when it is not acting! They are all a kind of feeling in the stomach area. You understand? But you have to be very observant.

I can't describe it now because I am not angry. No, I cannot become angry!

Q: Who is asking you to become angry?

M: No, I cannot become angry, there is nothing to be angry about. When anger comes, you can't produce anger, but sometimes it comes all the same. But before it is translated into action, if you are very observant, you will see it rising like a spark. Look at it and suddenly you will find that it is the same feeling as when you are jealous or when you have other emotions. It is the same thing, it's somewhere in the pit of the stomach, a heat! If you keep your attention there, that heat will spread all over your body. Then the anger's sting has been removed, and it is a beautiful thing.

This doesn't mean you should deliberately get angry and then feel it. I don't know how to deliberately get angry.

Q: You talk about letting it go, freeing your mind. The more I try, the more I remember things. Is there a process or technique to let it go?

M: Letting go is not a technique. Letting go is an understanding. Please understand this. The problem is that we have become so accustomed to techniques that we are always looking for new techniques. Technology and techniques. Letting go is not a technique, it's an attitude.

Let me give you an example. Suppose, I love music, it could be Indian music, it could be Western music, the great symphonies, Beethoven, Mozart, anything. If I love music, when I hear it, I get deeply absorbed in it. It's no effort on my part, it is an effortless absorption. When that happens, I automatically let go of everything else, nothing else exists except the music and there is no effort, except the effort to listen which is not a big effort.

This is roughly what I mean by letting go. It is not a technique. You become so serious that you don't want any support, and when you arrive at that point the supports fall off by themselves, because you realize that none of these techniques are going to help.

Q: Is 'thought' a problem and hindrance in inner mindfulness? It seems to me that 'thought' is the root cause of fragmentation and conflict. How does one handle this?

M: The first step is to be aware that it is so. To be aware that thought is interfering and that thought always divides. That's the first step. But that doesn't mean thoughtlessness! Please understand this. Thoughtlessness is an unconscious state.

The second step is we need to bring about a positive mind, from the negative to the positive. If you describe it in terms of tattvas, there is *tamo guna*, which is laziness, lethargy, *rajo guna*, which is active energy that results in activity and *sattva guna* which is tranquillity and balance. In sattva guna, the mind is all settled, calm, quiet and tranquil. In that state, perhaps, one is able to transcend thought.

But until you reach the sattva state, you need to move towards it by negating all the negatives, philosophically and psychologically. Shankaracharya did this by saying 'not this, not this', 'neti, neti'. He said, 'What I am seeking is not this, because it is still imperfect.'

Lastly, you reach a point where the mind has lost its poison, it's defanged. Then the mind itself takes you onto that which is beyond.

In the beginning there is always duality, no question. But in the end, it's over. At the last place, when you go to the last extent, all you can do is to let go.

While preparation is necessary—you have to fix the arrow on the bow and pull the string taut—if you want to hit the target, you have to let go of the string. Otherwise the arrow will stay where it is. While it's necessary to pull, you must also let go.

Q: As I start practising meditation, my mind retaliates and goes full-on, with more thoughts than before. Is this normal?

M: You are absolutely right. When you start moving away from the weather-beaten track and say 'I am finding a new path', then the mind gets very frightened and thinks, 'I am going to die.' So it will offer you various kinds of distractions and all the poison that was there will come out from inside. That's the time we have to be patient and say, 'It is okay. I know what's happening. Let it go.'

In ancient India, we have the story of the churning of the ocean, *samudra manthan*. It is a mythological story involving the devas, who are the good ones, and the asuras, who are the bad ones. You will see them in pictures and sculptures, it depicts the asuras with big moustaches, and the devas as clean-shaven.

The story is as follows: The asuras and devas decided to churn the primeval ocean, the ocean of milk. In order to do this, they found a snake called Vasuki, the snake that guards the God, Vishnu, which they used as the rope for the churning. And they found Mount Meru, which was used as the pole in the centre, around which the rope was wrapped. So, they put Mount Meru in the middle, put Vasuki around the mountain, one end was held by the devas, and the other end of the snake was held by the asuras. Poor snake! Then they churned the ocean.

Why did they decide to churn the ocean? They churned the ocean because they wanted the divine nectar of immortality. But when they churned the ocean, instead of getting nectar as they expected, the first thing that came out was poison, terrible poison, *halahala visham*.

When the poison came out, and Shiva saw that it was going to spread into the world, he is said to have swallowed it. As the poison was going down, his wife thought, 'Now my Shiva is going to die', so she held the throat and it became blue. When you go to Shiva temples you might have noticed that Shiva's throat is blue. Shiva is also known as Neelkanth, which means 'the one whose throat is blue'. This is a story. It is symbolic, of course.

What I am trying to say is that when the ocean was churned the first thing that came out was poison. In this way, when you start churning your mind, unless you have been a great soul for many lives, the first thing that comes out is poison. All the things that you did know, and all the things you did not know existed, will all come out. You need to get them out and throw them away. You can't subjugate them, they have to come out and go. It is like heating water, first there are bubbles, and then when they are released, it becomes vapour. It happens here in the same way. At that point you should not get discouraged. You shouldn't say, 'Oh I am such a dirty fellow.' No. You should say, 'Something is coming out of my mind.' It can't come out from anywhere else, right? Watch it. Allow it.

The Tibetans have a practice called meditation on the wrathful. In the Mahayana Buddhist tradition, there are two kinds of deities—deities that are peaceful and deities that are wrathful. The Tibetans have a practice called meditation on the wrathful deities. Let me tell you what they do.

First I visualize my own body and then I visualize that body as going into the void, becoming nothing. In its place comes the wrathful deity, have you seen those wrathful deities? Terrible looking fellows! So, I imagine that I have now become that wrathful deity, and all the wrath that is in me then comes out through this form. The door is shut, so I tear the pillows, I throw things, I become very wrathful. Then slowly, the wrath subsides. And instead of doing it to somebody else, I have done it to myself, alone, through this wrathful deity meditation. What's the result? Now, much of the poison has come off.

Next, the wrathful deity must be taken away, so the wrathful deity goes into the void, and the shape of my body returns. This is important at the end.

So there is nothing to worry about, this happens to everybody. It has even happened to me. Please, I didn't fall from heaven. I worked hard. You should work hard. Harder.

—Satsang with Sri M in the Alps, Day 4, 2018

7

MEDITATION AND DAILY LIFE

Q: I have a lot of family and work responsibilities and cannot find the time to sit down. What should I do?

M: I don't think it's a legitimate complaint. People have lots of work to do, but do they avoid movies? Do they not watch TV? Don't they play badminton? Don't they take their dogs out for a walk?

You can find the time, that's not the real issue. It means that you are not serious about meditation. You haven't realized how serious it is to do this. These are excuses. I don't accept the excuses. If you have to do it, you will do it anyhow. There is nothing like, 'I don't have the time.'

Q: I get easily distracted by sounds, the needs of my family, or other things in my surroundings, how should I handle this?

M: Let's talk about a practical way of doing this. In today's world, we cannot go into a cave and sit somewhere, that is not going to work.

I must tell you an interesting story related to this topic. When I was young, in Rishikesh in the foothills of the Himalayas, there was a man who came up to me and said, 'You know, I am fed up of Rishikesh.'

I said 'Why? I have just come here.'

He said, 'I'm fed up. There are too many ashrams, too many sadhus, too many people, too many pilgrims and too much noise.'

I asked, 'So what are you going to do?' I was sitting near the river, by the Ganga. I said, 'I think it is better than Delhi.'

He said, 'Yeah, but I don't like it. You know, I'm a man who loves solitude.'

I asked, 'So, where are you going?'

He said, 'Up, past Lakshman Jhula, I have heard that there is a cave. I'll go sit there and meditate.'

I said, 'Okay, may God be with you. Come back and tell me if something happens.' In those days I was also searching, I had not met my master, Babaji, at that point.

He went away and then three days later as I was sitting on the banks of the Ganga, I saw that he was back. I said, 'Hey, what happened?'

He said, 'What shall I say? I went there and sat in the cave for two days. I sat, and it was very nice. But there were mosquitoes.'

I said, 'Okay, and then what happened?'

He said, 'One day, I was in deep meditation, I thought I was in deep meditation, but then I open my eyes and there was an extra-terrestrial standing in front of me!'

I said, 'Wow this is great! Did he teach you anything?'

This man replied, 'Wait . . . Let me explain. It was not an extraterrestrial, it was a man from the municipality who had come to spray for mosquitoes.'

This is our situation. Don't assume you can go to the caves and sit down. It doesn't work. That said, you can make your own home, one room in your house, into your own private cave. In summer you can put on the air conditioning, and in the winter you can cover yourself with a blanket, and there you have your own cave. Nobody is going to spray you there, and nobody's going to come and disturb you. Nobody's going to come and say, 'You should come and join the ashram, become a member,' etc. You are free.

Find a place like that and then you can start your practice. Choose a place in your home where there is not much noise or disturbance and tell your relatives, 'I'm going to meditate for ten minutes, please don't disturb me, let me sit.'

Q: You mentioned that improper food and overeating interfere with meditation. Are there certain types of foods we should avoid?

M: Yes, there are *tamasic* foods that can make you sluggish and lethargic. This includes all meat and non-vegetarian foods, as they can make you lethargic. Fish is not so bad. But if you eat too much pork, you will sleep like a pig. If you eat beef, then you will sleep like a cow, and instead of Om, you will reverse it and say, 'Moo.' You know what I mean? You should avoid such foods as much as possible.

Eat light food. Avoid food which has too much fat.

Avoid food which takes too much energy to digest, because then all your energy goes into digesting. Even though you get your protein supply, the energy content is less and you will always want to sleep. So, eat light foods.

As far as spices are concerned, I won't comment, because sometimes spices keep you awake rather than put you to sleep. When I say *sattvic* food I'm not talking about bland food. Sattvic food basically means eating in moderation and eating the kind of food which does not make you sluggish.

Q: You said that being overweight can be linked to falling asleep in meditation. Do you recommend any specific types of physical activity?

M: Yes, if you are overweight, you should see according to medical standards, whether your weight is okay for your height and your age. If it's not, then you need to work on that to make it better and steady it a bit.

I don't know what exactly you need to be doing but you probably need more exercise and less food. A good deal of walking in the open air with a lot of oxygen. Drink water, do exercise. Yoga asanas are good too, but remember, yoga asanas are not only meant for making you slim. You might see a lot of people who do yoga asanas who are quite fat, so it's not about weight loss.

That said if you do rigorous yoga asanas you can lose weight. You can repeat each posture five times a day, especially the *surya namaskara* postures, even though you normally do surya namaskara once. But if you do surya namaskara five times, each posture, that will help you to reduce weight. You can also do other exercises like walking.

If you are overweight, then exercise is important. If you are very thin, then you don't need to exercise as much.

Q: I struggle with laziness and lack of discipline.

M: Discipline is a very general term because discipline can be good, and discipline can be bad. Discipline can be a pain in the neck and discipline can be enjoyable.

If you can turn discipline into an enjoyable thing, which means finding the reason why this discipline is going to help you improve or succeed, then discipline doesn't become mechanical. Discipline becomes difficult when it becomes mechanical because the mind reacts by saying, 'I don't want this control. I don't want this discipline. I just want to be free.' The irony is that you are disciplining your mind so that ultimately it blasts and becomes free forever. So, if you understand this, then you won't have a problem with discipline.

If your question about discipline is related to your work or other areas of life, then you will have to work it out. I can't tell you what to do in relation to that.

However, with regards to meditation, you should consider discipline as something that is ultimately going to free you from all discipline whatsoever. If you don't follow a discipline, you will still be stuck with some other discipline. It is inevitable in this world.

When you really look into something with complete attention, that itself is a discipline. It's not forced on you. That kind of discipline is essential. Because, I say, 'I can't see clearly, so I need to look', and I might use a telescope to look. That kind of discipline is essential. But if the discipline becomes, 'Every day at 9 a.m. I should look with a telescope', then some people might rebel against it.

That said, some may not rebel against such a discipline. When it comes to meditation, there are any number of different kinds of people on this earth, so you can't have a hard and fast rule that says,

'This is okay for everybody.' It doesn't work that way. You need to look at it on an individual basis and see what works. What suits one person need not suit another person.

That's why it is difficult. If there were some common formula then it would be a different matter, but there is no such common formula. In fact, I am personally very suspicious of common formulas. There cannot be common formulas because each person is made differently.

When somebody says, 'All you need to do is chant this name and you'll be free', I become quite suspicious. It can't be. Somebody may not like that name, then why should he chant it? It's like saying, 'This is the only way.' It can't be. Nothing is black and white. In this world, there are many grey areas and we need to handle it that way.

Q: I want to keep some part of my mind in meditation when I work, how can I do this?

M: That is very difficult, but you can attempt it. If you love the work you are doing, you can give complete attention to that work without distracting your mind, then it is like a meditation. If you don't like the work, then it is not easy.

People have the wrong idea, they believe that you can keep your mind distracted throughout the day but that you can sit without distraction for half an hour. This is not possible. If you apply your mind completely to whatever you are doing, then the mind learns to sit quietly when you are meditating. Now this is usually possible only if you love the work you are doing.

The whole theory of *karma yoga* is that you should work with complete attention for the benefit of others, rather than for your own self. Then the mind is in meditation and it becomes purified. This way, when you sit down to meditate, then your mind is already accustomed to being one-pointed.

In addition to this, when you are working, take breaks for short intervals, close your eyes and visualize, or do your japa, and go back to work. You can even sit at your desk for two minutes quietly. It is possible. If people ask, tell them, 'I am meditating.' Don't be shy. Don't be embarrassed. They might think you are a nutcase, but it is okay.

Q: Earlier, you mentioned about meditation with one-pointedness, ekagrata. Does it mean sitting alone and thinking about a single thing or can action, pravritti, become a one-pointed meditation?

M: Action, if done with single-pointed attention, becomes one-pointed meditation. But, usually, it is not done like this. It's usually not possible, it is difficult.

The founder of Zen Buddhism, Bodhidharma, he was from Thanjavur, in south India. It is he who took Buddhist teachings to China. There is a branch of Buddhism where meditation is given more importance. In China, it was promoted as 'dhyana Buddhism'. In Chinese, since they cannot say *dhyan*, it became Chan. When this Chan went to Japan, it became 'Zen'.

There is one Zen story which sheds light on this topic. A Zen master was living on a cliff in China. One day, three youngsters came searching for him after a lot of roaming. Tired and hungry, it was lunchtime when they reached and the Master was having soup. They told him that they had come to learn Zen. In Zen, the highest experience we call moksha, is referred to as *satori*. They expressed their wish to experience satori. The Master told them that he is having his soup. So, they kept quiet for a while. Then again, they asked for satori. And they got the same answer. When they asked a third time, then the Master called his attendant and told him to give them some soup. So, all of them had a bowl, a spoon and some soup. When they started to have it, they felt very foolish. They had come in search of satori, and now they were having soup.

So they asked again, and the Zen Master again said he is having his soup. They got angry and said, 'We are also having soup, are we not?' The Master said, 'This is the problem. I am having my soup. I am having my soup. I am having my soup. This is Zen. You are having your soup but thinking about Zen. That is not Zen.'

You asked about one-pointedness. In order to get one-pointedness, along with action, it must be work that we are interested in. It won't come when forced. If we are thus engaged in action, it is a meditation. It is dhyana. It is one-pointedness. But this state may not be sustained always.

For that, we can take some examples from different areas. Say, an artist, with complete inspiration, is painting. There won't be any other thought; it is a form of dhyana. When a poet writes poetry, his complete attention is in writing. This is dhyana. When a river is flowing and we are looking at it without any other thought, it is dhyana. This is a natural system of meditation.

However, when you are at work—amidst all sorts of distractions—and you still want to experience one-pointedness, then there are techniques. The technique is to couple the mind with some action. So we connect it with the action of breath. The mind cannot be without any action. It is like vacuum. We cannot maintain vacuum as air will immediately rush into it. Similarly, we cannot sit without any thought. Instead of focusing on thoughts from the outside, we substitute them with the thought of breath. In order to do this, when we inhale and exhale, we give full attention to the breath. Hence, the mind gets fully engaged but without thoughts from the outside. If this process is done for a while, the mind begins to cool down slowly, even though not fully. This is the beginning of dhyana.

Q: Is there a kriya or meditation technique that brings the amazing oneness experience when you're in activity, living life, when there is suffering around us?

M: Okay. So your basic question is, can kriya or meditation help you to strike this balance and sustain your sanity in the midst of the insanity around us?

All these techniques, kriya or any other form of meditation, are basically meant to do two things. First, it is to give the mind deep rest in the midst of all circumstances, and second is to activate the source of energy within us. We need tremendous energy to live in this tumultuous world and still keep our sanity. We need tremendous energy, but we dissipate our energies daily in petty, small things. Kriya has been found to be effective in activating the source of energy in us, so when that energy is active, then we have tremendous energy. It is gentle energy, not riotous energy.

Only when such energies are awakened in us, which is the function of kriya, can we maintain our sanity in the midst of this tumultuous world. The reason is, because we have so much energy, nothing can disturb us. If you live that way, I think you can change others as well. I know I explained it with a slightly different angle.

When we live in this world, the life energy in us, the prana, moves through 108 channels in the system. Roughly 108, this may not be an accurate figure. When we do one thing, it moves through one channel, if we are doing something else, perhaps it moves through a different channel. Since hundreds of things are taking place, the energy moving through all these channels is what keeps things going.

What the practice of kriya does is to gather all these energies which have been dissipated daily through all these multiple channels, and to bring them together to one place, not a physical place, but to bring them together so that you have the entire 100 megaton bomb ready with you. In a good way. It is for you to be able to use the energy so that your consciousness ascends from the gross to the subtle, subtler and subtlest, until it finally comes face to face with that which is our true essence. When that is discovered, there is no contradiction in living in this world and being in it.

Q: You talk about the importance of meditation to help us understand who we are. What if we already know our weaknesses without going within? I don't meditate.

M: That is because you have already gone inside. You have looked at yourself, otherwise you would never know your weaknesses.

Meditation is not just sitting with your eyes closed. That is not meditation. That can be meditation, but meditation is a very wide concept. You know the word meditation comes from an English word normally used for three processes. In the *Yoga Sutras*, which deal with meditation, it's divided into three parts, dharana, dhyana and samadhi.

Dharana can be with the eyes closed or eyes open. Dharana means the capability, capacity or practice by which one can put one's mind exclusively in one stream of thought. When that matures and goes on for some time, then that dharana becomes dhyana, it is a continuous process. When that dhyana goes on for some time, then you experience and understand what you are looking at, and that is samadhi.

If you are not practicing any particular mode of meditation, that doesn't mean that you are not the meditative type. There are people who do hours of meditation, sitting with closed eyes, but who are not able to put their mind into one stream, that is not meditation. It is only sitting down. There is still some advantage in sitting down, it calms the body, it calms the mind, but it may not be so deep.

Delving into your thought processes, delving into your mind, can also be a way to meditate, as it means to be increasingly aware of one's thoughts, how we perform actions, any prejudice that is present. It helps us see ourselves as we are. Then we know where to start the work.

Since we are dwelling on this particular theme, I want to tell you something else. If you really want to find out about yourself, to study yourself, the only way to do it is while you are in society. You cannot do it in a cave, it's not possible. It's nice to sometimes go and sit, everybody wants to have some quietness, but you need not have a cave. Your own house can be a cave, you can close the door and say don't disturb me and sit for a while, that's okay. But in order to understand where the mind has reached, how mature it is, what its characteristics are, how it reacts to situations, these can only be found out in communication, in social contact with the outside world. Otherwise there is no way you can know.

Hence, it's also important that one is aware of one's thoughts and actions while we are up and about doing our work in this world. It's very important.

8

PRACTICES THAT ASSIST WITH MEDITATION

Q: Do I need to learn kriya in order to meditate well?

M: No, you don't need to learn kriya in order to meditate. It's not as if all meditations are kriya-based. Meditation could simply be looking at a tree, going for a walk, sitting near the sea, or looking at the mountains and taking deep breaths. One doesn't necessarily need to practise kriya if what you mean by kriya is a technique.

There are lots of people who meditate but who don't know kriya. I'm talking about kriya as a technique. That said, we have found that kriya helps you to meditate, so if you learn kriya it might be easier for you to meditate. However, there is no such compulsion that you should know kriya in order to meditate. Even if you do kriya, in the end, you need to meditate without doing anything at all, because even kriya is an action. Finally, the goal is to be free of all action. So kriya is meant to free you from action through action.

Q: So kriya is like the thorn that is used to pull out the other thorn?

M: Yes. It's like the thorn which is used to pull the other thorn out. Finally nothing is required. You can also get hooked to kriya. Like any other addiction. It's a good addiction but ultimately you will discover the maxim, 'Let go and rejoice!' This is not to be mistaken with laziness. One might think, 'I'm so lazy I can't do kriya, so let go and rejoice!' No, that's not what I mean.

Q: I have heard that following the breath helps with meditation, how is the breath connected to the body and mind?

M: You know, among the most essential nourishments that is required for the body, the breath is the most important. You can live without food, you can live without water, but you can't live half a minute without breathing. Breath is so important.

Yet, we give no attention to the breath. From the time we are born, till the time we die, the breath is going on. You don't have to instruct yourself to breathe, you breathe automatically. But we don't give any respect or attention to this breath, which is the most important thing that nourishes life. We survive because of the breath and when it stops we are finished. The Gujaratis say, '*Off ho gaya*', 'It's gone off'. In Kerala they say 'puncture', if there is no air in the tyre you are done. The breath is so, so important, and yet we don't give any attention to this.

The breath is a link between your soul, your inner being and your outer body. If you can give attention to your breath, you can slowly move towards that which controls the breath. You don't actually control your breath, something else controls your breath, you may call it your parasympathetic nervous system or whatever, that controls your breath. As you give attention to the breath, you move towards that which is making your breath move up and down, and when you have touched that, then from there you trace it further to the inner, deeper levels.

This is the connection between the breath and the body. It's very important.

Many of us don't know how to breathe properly either, we do shallow breathing on the surface. Much of the diseases, even physical diseases, are caused because we do very shallow breathing. We don't breathe deeply enough. Somewhere along the line we have been taught that when you breathe, pull your stomach inside and expand your chest, so that you have an hour-glass figure.

When you want to breathe fully, you should push your breath down into the lower part of your lungs. That will not make your abdomen bulge, don't worry. In fact, it strengthens the muscle there. Full breathing is very important. Without oxygen even the brain cannot think clearly.

Q: Will following yama and niyama help me meditate?

M: Yes. You should follow, but more importantly one has to understand yama and niyamas.

The golden rule of yama and niyama is moderation. If you don't have moderation, you cannot meditate. Everything has to be done in moderate proportions—eating, drinking, entertainment, walking, exercising. There should be some control. If this can be followed, then one is following the basic yama and niyama. And of course, one has to stick to the truth.

Satya means reality or the truth. Satya is also beneficial to everyone. If something is true but it is not beneficial to everyone, then from the ultimate point of view it is not satya. Satya also means transparency. Often, we think one thing and say another thing. If we do that, then how can we see the reality? When you lead a false life twenty-four hours a day, you can't see reality. Satya also means not having desire for somebody else's wealth or possessions. If we are not satisfied with ourselves and keep looking for something more, then it becomes greed.

The rishis have said that to be truthful is to be transparent. If you yourself are not truthful, how can you teach truth to someone else? Truthful means to appreciate and encourage that part of reality which is beneficial to all as much as possible. If you don't practise this, you cannot expect the mind to be calm enough to meditate. It is not possible. This is why the yamas and niyamas exist. Now, pranayama involves the life energies, the prana, which are part of the system that connects intimately with the breath, the śvāsa. In pranayama, you can adjust the rhythms and patterns of the breath such that you get an undistracted mind. According to some, this undistracted mind is simply going back into the original state of 'non-distracted mind'.

On a related subject, with everything that we're discussing, it is actually my brain that is doing the thinking and talking. This thinking and talking is based on various experiences which the brain has gathered over the years from birth, or perhaps before birth, but let's leave the 'before', and look at the mind from birth onwards. The information and knowledge that I've acquired, the books that I have read, the love that I have gone through, the hatred I've experienced, the wonderful feelings, the heartbreaks, the whole gamut of human emotions that we live through—this makes our brain. We call it the mind. We cannot locate any other mind.

Now, we are saying that 'there is a mind which is free'. A brain that is kept free of all its hurt, all its regrets, all its anger, all its pretensions to knowledge, all the so-called knowledge which we have stuffed into it, which, of course, is in the past because it is based on the memories we have. Can we even conceive of a brain which has none of these? If you can, then that brain is not the brain any more, but the mind, the origin of consciousness.

Then, there is no moksha, there is no bondage, there is no freedom, there is nothing. All this bondage, these beliefs that 'I'm bound, I have to do this and that', it's all in this brain. If you can conceive, even for a second, of a brain which has none of these dead weights hanging on to it, positive and negative, a completely silent brain, in that silence is the original brain, which we can call the consciousness in the true sense of the term.

But until we get to that point we must practise yama and niyama.

I may be completely wrong, so I'm open to question. It's not some divine revelation, it's what I feel. I can be wrong, maybe I'm a nut. It is possible that I'm trying to make people nuts when they are really sane. I like these kinds of nuts.

Q: Is it easier to meditate at places such as ashrams or at a retreat where there are lots of people?

M: The reason why you find it easier to meditate at a retreat or in an ashram is because of the human mind's tendency to be caught up with what everybody else is doing. If you go into a nightclub and see people dancing, you also start dancing, right? The same effect applies to retreats, applies to places where people gather together, like in temples, and so on. It's the same thing but in a different way. You can say this is better than that. Yeah, that depends on what kind of person you are. Right?

For example, you open the door and walk into a club and at first you say, 'No, I don't want to dance, I'd prefer to sit down.' But there is heady music, you have a glass of wine and, before you know it, you are also dancing. This is the same thing that happens at a retreat, or a congregation, or when people sing and dance during a *kirtan* or *bhajan*, etc. It's the same thing but in a different form. I'm not saying it's good or bad; I'm not dismissing anything. I'm just saying that they are similar.

Q: I love listening to your satsangs, it makes me feel happy and more inspired to meditate. Can satsangs assist with meditation?

M: When I'm sitting here and we are talking about meditation, most of your minds are calm, collected and subtle. They are listening to this properly and understanding it—this itself is a kind of meditation. This kind of meditation is called a satsang. When a group of people put their minds together. You know the famous Rig Veda statement, '*Samvo manamsi jnanatam*'—'Together, with our minds, may we understand', this is a form of meditation.

It is a very important form of meditation, because when I'm alone, I may not be able to meditate because of my thoughts. They are not merely theoretical—they are things, actual things!

Hence, when I sit alone, I am disturbed by various thoughts because most other people are thinking about something else. They are thinking about the world; they are thinking about different things—so I find it difficult to meditate. But, when ten people are meditating together or thinking about the same subject, then I find it easier to meditate, because all thoughts are joining together.

This is the meaning of a satsang—which helps in meditation.

Q: I experience a lot of peace of mind in nature, is it okay if I spend time in nature?

M: You are able to meditate in some places because everything is quiet and there are no distractions. For example, you are able to meditate in a forest—assuming you are not afraid of being bitten or killed by wild animals—because it is very quiet, and you are in a different atmosphere. You are free of the usual distractions that come into your mind for some time and there is peace. When you are alone in the forest there is nothing there to distract you, there are birds singing but that is not a distraction, it makes you feel good.

Q: I enjoy meditating in places where sages and masters have been, should I spend more time in such places?

M: Why do you feel nice when you go to a place where people have meditated before? Because you have been *told* that people have meditated there before. If you're not told, a shepherd who goes and sits there probably won't meditate.

It all depends on the conditioning of your mind. You may also fall into a meditative state in the presence of someone meditating deeply, where you can be overpowered by the energy of that person. I personally don't think it matters where you meditate. A real yogi is one who can meditate anywhere, in a crowd, alone, and so on.

I'll give you an example, people go to Ramana Ashram to meditate because it has been drilled into their heads that Ramana Maharshi sat there for many years and that he was a free person. Not only is the belief present, but everyone talks about it as well. So, when you first sit down you temporarily feel happy thinking, 'Who am I? I am Ramana Maharshi'—but it's all the brain, the mind. When people go around and do *pradakshina* of the mountain, they feel, 'Ah it's so nice, Maharshi also walked this way.' What if nobody knew about it? There are animals, peasants and farmers who have been living there all their lives, yet they don't feel anything. It's all a question of what has been drilled into your head, and it reflects in what you do.

A yogi should be one, who, irrespective of any drilling, is able to feel it. He may be sitting in his kitchen and meditating, or he may be sitting in the slaughter-house meditating, without being affected. If this is possible, then you are a real yogi. Otherwise, most people get carried away with what can be roughly translated as mass hysteria or belief systems.

A yogi doesn't need any beliefs. A belief comes only when you don't know the reality.

I see the sun every day, I don't have to *believe* the sun is there, because I know it's there. The moment I *believe* it means that I *don't* know. I know the sun is there. When I know, I don't need any support. If I'm not sure, if I am on slippery ground, then I need to say, 'the Upanishads say it is true'. Because if I 'know' then I don't care what others say. Even if the Upanishads say it is not there, it is there! I'm not saying there is anything wrong with the Upanishads. They are the experiences of sages who have lived before and have experienced something.

We need to look carefully and not get drawn into mass hysteria. Hysteria is a big problem. When hysteria is built up, everybody's minds are at a high crescendo and when it is over sometimes they fall lower than they were before. If you enjoy it then go ahead but watch out. Heightened positive emotions are all right, however, the other side of heightened emotions is that afterwards the mind can plunge down to the lower depths. So, watch carefully.

This is why 'Sarvatra sama buddhaya' is a good expression. It means that 'in the midst of all, up or down, the mind remains tranquil—such a man is called a yogi'.

Q: When I listen to beautiful, devotional music, I am overcome with bliss, love and peace. Can music be an aid or form of meditation?

M: Music is a very, very important form of meditation and an adjunct to meditation. And again, you know it—I don't have to tell you that there are different kinds of music. There are many kinds of music which have no effect on meditation, are of no help, or rather, may be quite detrimental to meditation.

But there are forms of music which are conducive like bhajans, kirtans and also some very pure forms of classical music, melodies, and sometimes even ordinary, simple folk songs.

Once, I heard a very beautiful song. I was in Rishikesh, sitting on the banks of the Ganga. There was a boatman taking somebody across.

Generally boats don't cross after dark. It was full moon and he was crossing the Ganga, rowing his boat and singing in Garhwali. I couldn't understand the language. It was a simple song. The only thing I could hear was, 'Kanhaiya, Kanhaiya', but it was so beautiful. I don't think he even knew anything about music, it was his natural expression. Music is itself a discipline and there is a whole shastra on music.

As long as it contributes to your inner development, it is good. Sometimes, it so happens that it may not contribute to inner development because our aims may be different. But music certainly is a good form of sadhana.

Q: Does *moun* (silence) help to reach the inner state and what is *antarmoun* (inner silence)?

M: Silence helps in many ways.

First, what you are seeking cannot be expressed in words, so silence is a better expression. Second, when you don't talk, you save a lot of energy. A lot of our energy is spent talking. You conserve a lot of energy by not talking. Third, generally, when we open our mouths, we say unnecessary things. It is better to keep our mouths shut. These are all good indicators for being silent, at least as a discipline. Being silent and not talking for an hour a day is a great practice.

Now, what is inner silence?

This is a state and it cannot be practised. This naturally happens when you discover the essence of your being, and while you don't know how to express it, it is being enjoyed in silence. In this inner silence there are no multiple chaotic thoughts. Everything is quiet and peaceful.

Does external silence help in attaining inner silence? To a certain extent, only as it conserves energy spent in talking. But whether it reduces thoughts has to be seen, because if you mean quietening the inner dialogue when you say 'inner silence', it may not help. A dialogue may continue in your mind even if the outer is quiet. I may practise an hour of deliberate silence, but my mind is not in silence.

A truly silent mind is very rare.

Q: I have heard that meditation and purification of the mind go hand in hand. What does it involve, and how does one achieve a pure mind?

M: It's most difficult. It's easier said than done, but, there are certain ways and means that can help. All the great teachers from time immemorial have said that there are two strands which have to come together in one's spiritual progress for purifying the mind. One is how we live in this world and the other is what we do internally. Both things have to go side by side.

You cannot say that, 'I will lead as selfish a life I can. Every evening at seven I want to take a bath. I will watch TV all I like. And I won't care for my neighbour who is ill', and then after that continue to meditate for two hours a day to reach a pure mind. It is not possible.

So, there are two strands to this. All the great teachers, including Patanjali, said there are yamas and niyamas to be followed, and these are to be followed deliberately. Don't expect the mind to get purified by itself. You have to deliberately follow a way of life in which you cause the least harm to others. In fact, if possible, do good unto them.

The key is restraint. Control. Just before you speak, think: 'What am I going to say? Who am I going to say it to? Is this the right situation to say it?' You get good food, eat it, but always restrain yourself and say, 'Oh, maybe this could be shared by two?' Everything has to be a restraint in your daily life. If that kind of restraint is there, then slowly, the mind gets purified.

When you say purify, it's not as if the mind is dirty and it is getting purified. It is disturbed and distracted. It's ruffled. It's like a rollercoaster ride. You know how daily life goes. So, if you can become less self-centred, if you can practise self-restraint, if you can control your sense organs, at least to a great extent, then automatically the mind begins to become purified.

As a deliberate act of developing the mind, you should also find some time daily to sit down and internalize your mind. This is also important. These have to go side by side. Whatever work you do in the outside world, do it with one-pointed attention, otherwise you cannot expect to be one-pointed when you sit for fifteen minutes a day. The mind follows habit. You have established a pattern. You cannot suddenly shift it in the evening, right?

A yogi is one who drives when he drives and meditates when he meditates. He does not meditate when he drives. Then, he's a danger to himself and everybody on the road. Giving complete attention to whatever you are doing by itself is a meditation. You don't have to separate your meditation from this.

The guidelines are there in all religious texts, in all teachings. In Gujarat, there was this great saint called Narsinh Mehta; he sang beautiful Vaishnav songs. One of them says, 'A Vaishnav is one who thinks of others' problems as his own, and helps them to get out of their problems with the complete humility that he has done nothing.' This is the way to purify.

Q: I have heard you mention dhuni meditation, can you please tell us about that?

M: Amongst the Naths, there is a particular meditation called dhuni meditation, where you sit before the dhuni fire. I have done this sitting with my guru, Babaji. He could get the flame to go up or down as he wanted merely by thinking about it.

I have sat with him face-to-face, looking at the fire. It is very beautiful to meditate on the flame, especially at night. I was taught to completely open my eyes, watch the flame and then to close my eyes and visualize it inside. It's one of the most beautiful experiences. It burns off many of the 'leftovers' from our past, similar to how fire is physically a symbol of burning away all desires.

Only fire can do this. Fire can burn away everything. It also constantly reminds us that fire is the end. Of course, we can reach the same end with an electric crematorium, but the point is we will end in ashes.

When you watch the fire, the dhuni, you see how beautifully the flames come, how warm and nice the fire is. While all that is fine, you also see the wood burning, that you cannot hold onto the same log of wood, because it disintegrates, it's gone, it has become ashes. Fire illustrates time. As it moves, it doesn't spare anybody.

Babaji used to tell me, when you eat food, remember that time is eating you. No one can stop it. A few years ago you looked different in the mirror, now as you look again, you suddenly see some wrinkles creeping in. Time cannot stop. It moves, and it burns everything, including us, into ashes. This is why Shiva is always depicted with ash all over his body, which he takes from the cremation ground and smears on himself.

The Naths always take ash from the dhuni, and in public, they apply it on themselves. The Naga Babas—the *nangas*, the naked ones—always completely cover their body with ash. Smearing ash over one's body is a wonderful protection against the cold, and it demonstrates that, I believe, we are all going to be reduced to ash. 'I don't want anything, just give me a little food, that's more than enough.'

Fire is a great symbol of the spirit, and I personally feel that fire has a life of its own when it is lit. A fire is not an inanimate object, it has a life of its own which relates to you in a certain way. When you sit for long periods before a dhuni and meditate, if you meditate on the outer fire, it helps to light the inner fire.

Fire is a symbol of the spirit. Fire always burns up, it does not burn down. You can hold your fuel pointing downwards, but the fire will always burn upwards.

Meditating on the dhuni is also a symbol of the kundalini fire that burns inside, and through deep meditation lifts your consciousness to the higher realms.

Fire always has been a symbol of desire. Desire is a flame. Some people say they have been 'consumed by the fire', or have 'a fiery zeal'. Even anger is a kind of fire. In fact, all emotions, at their height, are fire. Suppose you see someone whom you were in love with in college, what do you say? 'My old flame.' You don't say, 'My old water', right? That flame, the igniting of the desire for the ultimate freedom, nirvana, is symbolized by the dhuni.

Everybody knows that a fire is fine when it stays where it is, but it can also be quite dangerous—it can burn the whole world down.

If you light one flame or one candle, it's enough to bring down the complete forest.

For *sadhaks*, spiritual aspirants, the most important thing to understand, is to light the inner fire that consumes all thoughts, other than the thought of reaching perfection. That is the central meaning of fire. And unless it is a fire, it's not going to work. Unless your enthusiasm is fired up, because you can't water your enthusiasm, it will not work. When one has decided that 'while all is well and fine, I've had enough and I have to move forward' that's the beginning of the desire for sadhana. Without that basic notion, sadhana doesn't work.

Q: Can you tell us about the meditation method that was taught by Ramana Maharshi? The method of seeking the 'I'.

M: Now Ramana Maharshi's way is not everyone's cup of tea.

In Ramana Maharshi's case, while he was still young, he had an experience which did not happen in meditation. He was doing nothing. I ascribe this to his having meditated in many lives. Anyway, it doesn't matter. He had an experience where he actually found himself to be not the body, to be disassociated from the body. That stuck in his mind and he said, 'If this is not true, if I am not this body, then who am I?' That's where his enquiry started.

Now we haven't had any such experience, so we must start the inquiry first and then go on. We have to say that 'Ramana Maharshi had this experience where he found that he was not the body. Even though I don't have that experience, I think that he was a genuine person and a great yogi, and he did have that experience. Then, asking the question "Who am I" if not the body, he reached the goal.'

In simple words, what Ramana Maharshi said was, 'I am not the clothes that I wear, because if I take them off and hang them up it is clear that I'm not the clothes. But when I wear the clothes it looks like the clothes are part of me. But then what am I?' That was his question. With great attention he meditated on this until he hit upon his true essence.

However, it's not so easy to follow this line of inquiry in the world where we live, with so many distractions. If you read some of the teachings of Ramana Maharshi, he himself says that if you can't do that inquiry, at least watch your breath. 'At least', he uses the words 'at least', watch your breath. The reason for this is because when you're watching the breath, you slowly go within and begin to realize, 'What am I? Am I this mind or is there something behind it?' And Ramana Maharshi found it.

There is no question in my mind that he found what we are looking for. And when he found it, he found that which is inside, which is the true essence of being, is also outside. You will rarely see a single picture of Ramana Maharshi with his eyes closed, because for him the inside and the outside were not demarcated. But he had to find it inside first. He did perhaps in the early days close his eyes but then he found that everything was one.

9

GRACE AND GURU FOR MEDITATION

GRACE AND GURU FOR MEDITATION

Q: Does someone need grace or a teacher in order to be able to meditate?

M: Yes and no.

You may need a teacher to guide you on the right way of doing it. But you don't have to have 'grace'. Grace doesn't come when you seek grace. It is something that is spontaneous. I want grace. In fact, grace 'abhors' the word grace. It's completely spontaneous. You can't define it. You can't 'work for grace' because grace is spontaneous.

Sometimes you may be a terrible fellow, but grace is there. Sometimes you may be saintly, but there is no grace. So that word 'grace' is very misleading. Grace is something which is always there. But, sometimes, we don't feel it depending on how open our mind is. For meditation or doing your practices, you don't really need grace, you need hard work.

I would say, 'Yes, somebody can instruct you' but that teacher should have a rough idea of your psyche so that he can guide you accordingly.

In the *Yoga Sutras* of Patanjali, they talk about *ishwara* or the supreme from whom the grace comes. The term ishwara means the primordial free being, more so than a supernatural being. The primordial being is a being who is free from all conditioning, and the essence of that is also in every individual. When we free ourselves from all conditioning, we are ishwara. See that? So ishwara and grace are not something external coming from somewhere out there. It's internal.

Q: You said grace is everywhere, always there, you have to have an open mind.

M: Open mind. What does an open mind mean? A brain free of all dross. Then you will see that grace is there, you don't have to 'find' it anywhere.

Q: So, it is not 'believing' in something that is there and trying to find it?

M: That is a belief system. While you may hold that belief system, you should simultaneously keep your mind aware that 'this is my belief system'. Maybe I am happy with this belief system for now, but when all beliefs are gone and there is no more carrying of all these memories, expectations, greed, etc., when all these things have subsided in the brain, only then will we know the true nature of the mind. And that mind doesn't need grace. That mind is grace itself.

Fortunately, anybody who has touched it feels that it is like a circle with its circumference everywhere and its centre nowhere. Even the word 'vast' cannot define it. Everything must go. You may live in this world, but people may think this fellow is strange.

Q: Reaching the spiritual goal, is it a matter of time or effort or grace?

M: Is it a matter of time? Is it a matter of effort? Or is it a matter of grace?

All the three. It is a matter of effort, it is a matter of time and it is a matter of grace.

I will tell you how it goes. I am convinced that without there being some grace, there can be no effort. If you see somebody making some effort towards this, there is already grace, so forget about that question. Grace is already there. Otherwise it's impossible to even look in this direction.

Now, once that is there, effort begins. Once effort begins, there are many factors involved, 'Who is the person who is doing the effort?' 'What is the material he has at the moment with him?' 'What is his background?' 'How much effort has been made in the past?' Depending on the answers to these questions, the time is decided.

Suppose the seed is already a mature seed, ready to sprout, then it takes a little less time. If it is not, it takes a little more time. But grace is already there from the beginning.

Grace is like the gentle, fragrant breeze. All effort, all sadhana is the attempt to keep your doors and windows open so that when the breeze gently blows, it enters the room without any resistance. It is always there but you cannot dictate when it is going to blow in. If the windows and doors are shut, it can't enter. So put all your effort into seeing that the windows and doors are open and welcome grace when it wafts in, with humility.

ACKNOWLEDGEMENTS

I acknowledge the fact that without the blessings of Sri Guru Babaji and my personal teacher Maheshwarnath Babaji I would have learnt nothing about meditation. I am also thankful to the great beings I met subsequently who taught me the finer points of what meditation is and how to meditate.

NOTES